A Life of Two Halves
The Chris Garland Story

Dedicated to my mum, who has always been there for me.

A Life of Two Halves
The Chris Garland Story

Chris Garland
with James Ryan and Mark Leesdad

Foreword by Ian Botham

 *redcliffe*

First published in 2008 by Redcliffe Press Ltd.,
81g Pembroke Road, Bristol BS8 3EA

www.redcliffepress.co.uk
info@redcliffepress.co.uk

ISBN 978-1-906593-11-7

British Library Cataloguing-in-Publication Data
A catalogue record for this book is available from the British Library

Cover design by Mark Cavanagh
Typeset by Harper Phototypesetters Ltd, Northampton
Printed and bound by MPG Books Ltd, Bodmin, Cornwall

CONTENTS

Photographs between pages 52–53 and pages 116–117

ACKNOWLEDGEMENTS

Throughout this book I have tried to give credit to the many people who have supported me throughout my life. If I've left anyone out, my apologies.

On the footballing front, people like Bristol City manager Fred Ford and team legend John Atyeo were both tremendous influences and people I admired and respected enormously. Also, it's not that often that members of the media get a 'thank you', but journalists David Foot, Peter Godsiff, Graham Russell, the late Chris 'Crash' Lander and Herbie Gillam usually gave me a very fair press, as I made my way in the game.

To all my family and friends who have been there for me – thank you.

Finally, to writers James Ryan and Mark Leesdad, who have guided me through the choppy waters and minefields of, as Mark calls it, 'wordsmithing,' thanks.

Footnote: Many of the photographs used have come from my personal collection, from childhood through to the present day. A lot of my playing days' pictures came from that collection, many given to me by journalists, and I have tried, where humanly possible, to ensure that copyright has not been breached.

FOREWORD

It is fitting in many ways that my personal friendship with Chris developed as a result of a mutual friend. Pete 'Jock' McCombe, like many fans in the West Country at the time, followed Bristol City during the football season, and came to watch Somerset County Cricket Club during the warmer months. During the late 1970s, City were in the old First Division, and Jock took Viv Richards and me along to Ashton Gate. He knew most of the boys, but was particularly good friends with Gerry Gow and Chris, who was affectionately known as 'Tutch'.

My memories of Chris stretch back further than these initial 'social' meetings. As a youngster, the Chelsea side was very much a passion of mine, with the likes of Peter Osgood, Ian Hutchinson and, of course, Chris. It was a privilege to play for the 'old' Chelsea boys in Ron Harris' testimonial match at Stamford Bridge against the then present Chelsea line-up. We won 1-0 and the winning goal came courtesy of a wonderful move down the left-hand side. Incidentally, I was on the left of midfield, but as you can imagine, I rarely talk about it!

Socially we had some great times and Tutch was usually central to everything going on. Somerset were on the crest of a wave and he became one of the boys, along with a few of the City players, such as Gerry Gow and Len Bond. There was quite an affiliation between the two camps at that time.

I remember times when Chris and I used to visit Peter Osgood and Ian Hutchinson at their pub in Taunton, and really play them up. We would send back single chips if they weren't up to scratch, but it was all just a continuation of the dressing room banter that we all enjoyed during our playing days. I'm sure Chris would agree with me when I say that when you finish playing, it is not necessarily the game that you miss, but the humour in the dressing room, all of which he and I were very much a part. Chris would constantly be at the forefront of the dressing room entertainment, yet would always subsequently deny any involvement. It is something that is almost impossible to explain unless you have been involved.

It was a few years later that our relationship had appeared to have gone full circle. Chris always turned up to support me and the lads at Taunton, and I also enjoyed watching Chris – despite his somewhat dodgy mullet haircut! In an attempt to improve my fitness, I went to Scunthorpe United and, having impressed in training, was invited to play for the reserves and subsequently the first team, much to the delight of the powers-that-be at Lords! I then went on loan to Yeovil Town for one month, much to the delight of my wife Kath! Ironically, it was Chris, under Gerry Gow's management at Yeovil, who had to strap up my left ankle before I went out to play. I have to say that he was bloody awful at it and took great pleasure in ripping off at least four acres of hair! After the game, Chris often made reference to my wage packet hitting the ground with a thud at Yeovil, whilst his would float to the floor – the reason being, mine was full of coins!

Chris was a fantastically gifted footballer, who probably never reached the heights that his ability should have allowed. I remember him being a tremendous team-player and fantastic on the ball, although physically he had the pain threshold of a gnat hitting a windscreen!

Chris has always had a wonderfully generous character, and would do absolutely anything for anyone. He came along and took part in my charity walks for leukaemia, this time supporting me in a very personal crusade. That is the great thing about sport, you can have friendships that are three days old or thirty years old. Either way, sportsmen tend to click, and Tutch and I got on extremely well from the beginning. We always had the understanding that I would have the last word on cricket, whilst he would have the final say on football.

Chris has always been, and always will be, a true friend.

IAN BOTHAM

INTRODUCTION

Football, and in particular, Bristol City Football Club, became a way of life for me from a very early age. Ashton Gate was within a short goal kick from the family home in Ashton Vale, and from the age of five or six, a football became my constant companion.

My love for Bristol City developed into almost an obsession. Collecting newspaper cuttings about the club was a daily event, and more often than not, one man stood head and shoulders above the rest in the eyes of the West Country media.

The 'head and shoulders' analogy was a phrase long to be associated with John Atyeo. Although metaphorically referring to his performances on the pitch, his physical presence and attitude towards the game, and life in general, made him a legend with the Ashton Gate faithful, not to mention an idol in the eyes of an impressionable youngster seeking to emulate him in every way. As well as reading about the great man whenever I could, I also started collecting autographs, and used to hang around the players' entrance at the ground, waiting for the team to emerge. I was grateful for any signatures at the time, but there was only ever one player that I was really waiting for.

One afternoon at the age of nine, I finished lessons at South Street Primary School and ran to the ground on one of my player-seeking missions, only to come face-to-face with John Atyeo himself. I knew immediately that I wanted to be everything he represented: a fantastic footballer, a great presence and above all, a gentleman. When he ran onto the field, he was the most magnificent figure of a man, with the respect of everyone around him, and you always had the expectation that something was about to happen. John's record for Bristol City speaks for itself, 351 goals in 645 appearances, and it is fair to say that it will never be beaten.

My Saturday mornings were spent playing football for the South Street's school team at the nearby Clanage Playing Fields – overlooked by the imposing grounds of Ashton Court on one side, with Bedminster Cricket Club (once the spiritual home of the legendary W.G. Grace) adjoining, and the beauty of the Clifton Suspension Bridge dominating the western skyline. Despite taking it somewhat for granted at the time, I now realise what a terrific place The Clanage was to play football. It became almost a ritual every Saturday. From there, we would go straight to Greville Smyth Park (Ashton Park to the locals), and kick a ball about in the nets until it was kick-off time across the road at Ashton Gate. In reality, kick-off was something we very rarely witnessed. With money scarce for such entertainment, it was always a case of 'how we were going to get in?' We had to either wangle our way past the doorman, wait until half-time for them to let us in for free, or go and watch the reserves play. During the 1950s, City regularly attracted crowds of over two thousand for reserve team matches, but despite it being football, and Bristol City at that, there was something – or rather someone – missing. The chances of John Atyeo turning out for the reserves were about as likely as me pulling on a blue-and-white quartered jersey and catching the next bus to Eastville. Whatever the outcome, first eleven or reserves, along with most of the other lads south of the river, Saturdays for me were completely dedicated to football.

As I developed, both physically and mentally as a footballer, it became clear that my style of play could never be based on 'Big John's' physical attributes. He was a centre-forward in every sense of the word, and I was a good four or five inches shorter and two stones lighter. Despite progressing into an inside forward, I learnt quickly that the basic qualities of football professionalism remain the same. Whether it was watching him from the terraces, or later on when I became an apprentice under him and seeing him train at first hand, I was always looking to learn from his wealth of knowledge.

It was a fantastic experience for me when I signed apprentice forms at Bristol City in August of 1964, at the age of fifteen. The biggest part of my day was spent cleaning the dressing rooms and sweeping the terraces, but to have John Atyeo walk into the same boot room as me made the hairs on the back of my neck stand up. I eventually had to clean his boots, which was an honour for me, although unfortunately they were the size of wellingtons! The process of cleaning, waxing and dubbing them seemed to take forever, but I didn't mind one bit. Tipping his apprentice wasn't John's strong point, though; he was one of the tight ones and if you got a penny out of him you counted yourself lucky!

As I joined the club as an up-and-coming youngster, John was coming to the end of his wonderful career at Ashton Gate, but he gave me one particular piece of advice which stood me in good stead for my entire career. Just outside the changing rooms at Ashton Gate, there were some old-fashioned toilets made of breeze blocks, with a goal painted on one wall. In the top left-hand corner was a black spot, with a red spot in the opposite corner. John told me that if I had any spare time, not to waste it, but to come back to the wall alone and practise striking the ball with both feet, aiming to hit the target 'spots' in either corner. He was right – although it didn't seem a lot at the time, I saw an amazing amount of improvement in my game and I continued to follow that advice for years to come.

My testimonial match against Manchester United in 1993 was a fantastic occasion. John was first on my ticket list and I was delighted when he accepted my invitation. Marina Dolman, wife of the late Harry Dolman who did so much for the club during his years as chairman, once recalled how she saw John cry on only four occasions: on scoring City's second goal against Oldham in 1965 which secured promotion to Division Two; when the Ashton Gate crowd gave him one final standing ovation on his retirement; after the funeral of his close friend Harry Dolman; and when I, Chris Garland, told him that he had been my schoolboy hero. With all the words in the English language, a greater tribute could never have been paid to me.

John's death, only one month after my testimonial, was a very sad time for everyone who knew him, and there was a tremendous turn out for his service of remembrance. I attended the service with ex-City players Alan Williams and Jantzen Derrick. The number of people wishing to pay their final respects, both inside and outside, showed the respect he had earned and the impact he had made on people's lives during his own lifetime. Although there is now a stand named after him at his spiritual home of Ashton Gate, he once told me that he felt as though he wasn't welcome at the club after his retirement. For a man who did so much for Bristol City Football Club, and put them on the map, he should have received life membership, the freedom of the club, and of course, been made to feel welcome.

His encouragement, example, loyalty and influence will live with me forever, and to John Atyeo, I will be eternally grateful. He was the man who first got me interested in football, kept me interested in football, and helped me to develop as a man both on and off the pitch. There will never be anyone quite like him, and in my eyes, he will always be 'Mr. Bristol City'.

CHAPTER ONE

THE STREETS TO THE CITY

As far as introductions go, it was unremarkable. It came three weeks after it should have done, and when it was all over, there was plenty of celebration, although I missed the party because I was still in hospital. Whilst I was the centre of attention, there were no thoughts on my father's part of me playing for England and it all went off unnoticed by the local media. I suppose it does sound uneventful, but it was early days, and this was just the first of what would prove to be several important debuts during my life.

The venue was Southmead Hospital, Bristol, on 24 April 1949. Following the birth of my brother Martin four years previously, I was the second son to Grace and George William Henry (known as Bill to family and friends). Weighing in at $8^1/2$ lbs. and arriving three weeks late, it seemed that even then I wanted my appearance to be memorable – my mother just thought I was lazy!

My first real recollections of life are four or five years later, and, after spending a short time living with my grandparents, are memories of living in Ashton Vale. It was in Ashton Vale, a small district in south Bristol, that I went to primary school. The family lived in what was then supposed to be a temporary prefabricated house. It was one of a number in the area built during wartime as convenient and affordable accommodation, as Bristol as a city had suffered more than most at the hands of the Luftwaffe. The notion of durability can be added to those of convenience and affordability, as the house is still standing today, some sixty years later, and is still a place I often visit.

My father was a lorry driver for all his life. He worked tirelessly to provide for my mother, Martin and me, and would frequently be away from home, driving the length of pre-motorway England. My mother also worked, often arranging flexible hours of work around Martin and me. She worked part-time for the tobacco manufacturers W D & H O Wills for twenty-five years. Wills were a major employer in south

Bristol throughout the 19th, 20th and into the 21st century, though later under the title Imperial Tobacco Limited.

Ashton Vale was a wonderful place to grow up. It seemed to be a part of the countryside, which I loved, yet was close enough to the hustle and bustle of the big city. On a weekend, as many as ten of us would march down to Hancock's Woods, over what the locals had nicknamed 'The Black Bridge'. It was here that I had my first real taste of football. We would take a ball with us, flatten the wild, usually overgrown grass, and play for what seemed like hours. This was often carried over into playtimes at Ashton Vale Primary School, when the likes of Keith and Colin Moore were at the forefront of playtime matches. Colin was the same age as my brother Martin, whilst Keith was my age, and like Martin and me, both were football fanatics.

There was one thing at school that would guarantee credibility and respect from just about all the lads, not to mention the freedom of the playground – whoever brought the ball into school was the boy everyone wanted to know. It was often a case of whoever could afford to bring the ball into school was the 'top boy', and as a result, it was very rarely me.

On one particular occasion, we were having our customary playtime kick-about, when one of the older boys stole our ball. It was around this time that, because of my somewhat slight build, my father told me I had to start standing up for myself. I will always remember the lad who took the ball. He was named 'Slough', a monster who was at least twice my size, and always wore large boots, seemingly to emphasise his superior frame. I went to grab the ball back from him, but at the same time he went to kick it, missed, and kicked me under my chin, nearly chopping my tongue in half. I was rushed to the hospital, almost as quick as my mum dashed round to offer her views on the matter to his parents. I've still got the scar today, but it taught me an early lesson on the importance, and dangers, of standing up for myself!

My time at Ashton Vale Primary was relatively short-lived, and when I was nine, the family moved a mile up the road to Brighton Crescent, Parson Street. I then attended South Street Primary School in Bedminster, and it was here that I realised my fanaticism with football, and in particular, Bristol City Football Club. I was fortunate in that the other kids in the area shared my love, and used to stay out until all hours, playing football underneath the street lamps, with gates at either end doubling as goalposts. Otherwise we would simply sit on the kerb edge and talk about football for hours. Moving to South Street was the best possible move for me in footballing terms, and it was here that I met boys of a like mind. I was also lucky to have some good players around me to play with and learn from, even at that young age. Roger Oldfield had a great left foot and would take tremendous corners and set pieces, whilst Keith Treasure would go on to play for Bristol Boys. As well as sharing a passion for playing the game, we also loved watching Bristol City.

We all had similar heroes at Ashton Gate, and little did we know that the names we idolised then would go on to become legends in the history of Bristol City Football Club. John Atyeo, Tony Cook, and later on Jantzen Derrick, Bobby 'Shadow' Williams and Brian Clark were just a few of the players whose footsteps each and every one of us wanted to follow. John Atyeo was an incredible centre-forward and his record would be phenomenal in any era, whilst Tony Cook, who unfortunately has also passed away, was one of Bristol City's truly great goalkeepers. One player who certainly should have progressed further in the game was Jantzen Derrick. He had an abundance of talent and more skill than I ever had, but, as Jantzen himself would often say after a match, 'has it been a good day or a bad day?' I still meet up with Jantzen and he hasn't changed a bit since his playing days. He is still the same nice guy, but in the often cut-throat world of professional football, it is regrettable that this may well have been his downfall. Later in my career, I would actually see myself more as a Brian Clark than a 'Shadow' Williams. Like Brian, I had to work hard to improve my game, whilst the likes of Shadow and Jantzen had great natural ability.

Despite having Bristol City permanently in our blood before we reached double figures, it seemed that most of the boys in the area felt it necessary also to follow a First Division team. I didn't have this urge, especially as City had gained promotion from the old Third Division (South) as champions a few years earlier, in the 1954-55 campaign. City were back in the Second Division after an absence of twenty-two years and in doing so had equalled Nottingham Forest's record in the Division of seventy points and thirty wins.

Bristol City were capable of pushing for promotion to the First Division themselves, and this was more than enough for me. However, what happened in February 1958 showed me the profound effect that football can have on life, and made me think about more than just the game on the pitch. The Munich Air Disaster brought Manchester United Football Club into the hearts and homes of many people. Losing so many lives, many young, and all of them talented, affected not just the footballing world but the whole nation. It was as a result of that terrible accident, and the way the club returned after losing so many great players and staff to win the European Cup, that I adopted Manchester United as my 'other team.' Although Bristol City had always, and has always, been the only team I needed, there has always been a special place in my heart for Manchester United.

South Street Primary School gave me my first real taste of playing competitive football. I use the words 'real taste' carefully, as even a meaningless playground game could turn into the most competitive of matches for a group of nine-year-olds. Nevertheless, like the rest of the football-mad boys in the school, my ultimate aim was to play for the school team, against all the other schools in the area. In the run-up to Christmas in 1958, aged nine, I realised that to stand a better chance of playing for the school team, I would need my own pair of football boots. Thankfully, my father had spotted my enthusiasm and passion for football and on Christmas morning I realised my letter to Father Christmas had been answered. I was fortunate enough to be picked for the team shortly after and it gave me great pleasure to compete with the likes of Ashton Gate School, Marksbury Road School and Hareclive School to name but a few. Playing away in areas of Bristol such as Hartcliffe and Knowle West was an intimidating experience, and getting to the game was often difficult enough. Then if you won the game, it was extremely doubtful whether you would get the bus home! Even getting back to my mum and dad's from home games was often a problem, and it always seemed to be me fighting with someone from another school. However, it gave me the opportunity early on to see how I compared to lads of the same age in south Bristol. Initially I probably stood out at the age of nine or ten because I was what was classed as 'a greedy little sod!' I loved to have the ball at my feet, but enjoyed scoring goals even more. At that early age, I couldn't understand the need to pass the ball, when I could do it all myself – needless to say, with the 'help' of those around me, I grew out of that fairly quickly! I was a relatively quiet child and rarely expressed my feelings, so as with my first pair of boots, it was left to my dad to spot my real love of playing football. My mother had been single-handedly brought up by her mother, and didn't have a father figure in her life until the age of fourteen when her mother remarried. With no brothers, sport, and football in particular, simply played little part in her life – until now. At first she wasn't at all happy with the amount of time I dedicated to football, and even paid an impromptu visit to the school, complaining that she sent her son to school to learn arithmetic and how to read and write – not to play football. Thankfully they reached an amicable agreement whereby I could continue playing football, providing I did well in my academic studies. It goes without saying that this was all the incentive I required, and I worked hard at school, which undoubtedly stood me in good stead for life outside of football. My mum realised soon afterwards that football had rapidly become the focal point of my life and would be something she would have to take an interest in, otherwise conversations in our house would be limited, to say the least. As dad often worked away, mum started to come over to The Clanage to watch me play and fell in love with the game immediately. From then on, she watched me whenever she could and this would continue throughout my life, something for which I am extremely thankful.

We were lucky enough to have a fairly successful team, and, in only my second year at the school, I was top scorer with over fifty goals, breaking the existing record. Luckily for me personally, and for the team, my record continued into the following season, and Mr. Vokes, our sportsmaster, made me captain, which I considered to be a great honour. Arthur Vokes was heavily involved in the local junior football scene. As well as being a great teacher and influence on all the boys at South Street, he was chairman of the Bristol Schools FA, and went on to be a member of the selection committee. I owe much of my early development to him, a man who knew the game of football intimately, and had the gift of being able to communicate his knowledge in a language we all understood and acted upon. I remember one particularly memorable occasion when I scored ten goals in an 11-1 win over Bishopsworth at the Clanage, our home pitch. It was around this time that my goals started to make the local press, and as a result, my name became familiar to many involved with football in the Bristol area. It was probably a combination of my parents' support, my performances on the pitch, and the press coverage, that I was selected to attend trials for the Bristol Junior Boys team. The trials were on a Tuesday afternoon at the Clanage, and I turned up along with twenty-four other lads, eager to make an impression on the selectors. My biggest problem then wasn't necessarily whether I was good enough, but more a case of whether my size would count against me. I was very slight with a crew-cut, and everyone said I was too short to make it as a footballer. Some people even say the same today, but the truth of the matter is that if you're good enough, you're big enough – and following the trial, I'm glad to say that, in this instance, size really didn't matter! It was the start of a very special period for me. Following a successful year with South Street and the Bristol Boys team – when we played at grounds such as Twerton Park, Bath, and The County Ground, Swindon – I was also made captain of the Bristol Junior Boys team during my final year at South Street. It was a perfect ending to my time at junior school, and it paved the way as I progressed to secondary education.

Moving to secondary school is a big step at the best of times, and I was dreading that I might have to move on to Ashton Park Secondary School. It was a local school, with the Clanage across the road, and my brother Martin had started there four years previously. My ill-feeling towards the school was simple: they played no football at all. Ashton Park was a rugby school, and the thought of not playing football put me off once and for all. Luckily for me, my parents allowed me to attend Southville Secondary School. The school was sited closer to the family home and sat in the shadows of the Wills tobacco factories which lined Raleigh Road. Mum and dad were too busy earning a living to realise whether I was a good player or not, whilst academic reputation was the last thing on my mind – I just wanted to play football. The school had just two teams – an under-13s and an under-15s team. At the age of eleven or twelve, you were obviously competing with older and stronger boys for places in the starting line-up, and with my size being a hindrance in my own age group, this was a disadvantage I could have done without. However, my determination paid off, and I was selected for the under-13s team straight away. Mr Templar and Mr Williamson, the latter a season-ticket holder at Ashton Gate, were sportsmasters at Southville and, similarly to Mr Vokes at South Street, were a tremendous influence on me, and offered encouragement in developing my game.

Once again, at Southville I was fortunate enough to be surrounded by good-quality players, enabling me to learn and improve constantly. Steve Carey was one such player who, although he has now lived in

Oslo for twenty-five years, and is closer to Martin's age, is still a good friend of mine today. Steve's example was typical of several lads that I grew up with. He had trials with Arsenal as a youngster, and along with the likes of John Bishop, Phil Thomas and Ray Collins, had fantastic ability, and would go on to play a good standard of amateur football. Maybe with an extra push or shove in the right direction those lads could have made it into the professional ranks, but the key factor is that you have really got to want it. It is a lot of hard work, and as a youngster, you have to make sacrifices. The problem with many teenage lads then – and I'm sure it is no different today – is that you want to go out with friends and meet girls. Consequently, many talented players fall by the way-side, not because they aren't good enough, but because of circumstances off the field. Even at that stage, you have got to be dedicated from an early age.

I progressed to the senior Bristol Boys teams and in the process played good teams at some of the country's leading league grounds. These included Aston Boys at Villa Park, Cardiff Boys at Ninian Park and various teams on several occasions at one of our home grounds, Eastville, then home of Bristol Rovers. Although Eastville was just another ground, I felt nothing 'homely' about it at all. Playing there was one thing, but then I just wanted to get out of the bloody ground as quickly as possible. I achieved one of my first dreams on 27 September 1963, at the age of fourteen, when I played at Ashton Gate. The fixture was against Newport Boys, and I was incredibly nervous, but scored two goals and played well in a 6-2 victory. It was a memorable occasion, and scoring two goals, as well as grabbing the headlines in the local papers the next day, really put the icing on the cake. It became a regular occurrence for me, and I went on to play Swindon Boys and Liverpool Boys on the hallowed turf, that the locals would later nickname 'The Wembley of the West'. It wasn't just with Bristol Boys that I appeared at Ashton Gate that year. Southville reached the final of the Woodcock Shield for the first time in its history. The Woodcock Shield was the main cup competition for secondary schools in Bristol, and the final was played at the home of Bristol City. We drew 2-2 with Hartcliffe School and shared the trophy for six months each, as bad light meant extra-time was not possible. It was a fantastic achievement for Mr. Williamson and Mr. Templar, and just reward for all of their hard work.

The 1963–64 season had already become somewhat overwhelming in footballing terms, and in addition we also moved house again, this time to Ashton and literally overlooking Ashton Gate. Our new home was Winterstoke House, a block of flats on Duckmoor Road, later to become famous as Nelson Mandela House in the hit TV comedy series 'Only Fools And Horses'. In the days before the Dolman Stand was built, it was the perfect vantage point to watch my heroes in action. At first I was a little sceptical about moving from a house into a block of flats. But with football to watch on my doorstep, and a park to play in around the corner, I soon came to realise that the move was for the best – and mainly for my benefit. As far as I was concerned, the season couldn't get any better, but there were still two unforgettable experiences to come. These would exceed all my wildest hopes and dreams, and form the foundations for the rest of my life.

The first came when I was called up for the English Schools Football Association trials, as a result of my performances for Southville and Bristol Boys. I travelled down to the Cricklefield Athletic Ground, Ilford, on Saturday 25 January 1964, and played in a South East of England versus South West of England fixture. It was strange for a young lad like me to venture to London, and I'm sure the expectations from the natives were that I would turn up in a straw hat, with the characteristics and accent of a farmer. Once again, if nothing else, it was an exercise in character building, but I was, and always have been, proud to come from Bristol, so prejudice was the last thing on my mind going in to the trials. The South East of England team included two names that would go on to play at the highest level in English football, in Trevor Brooking and Steve Kember. Even at that early stage in their careers, their quality stood out, in company regarded as some of the finest players in the country in that age bracket. I felt as though I played relatively well despite only playing for around thirty minutes. Nevertheless, Mr. Williamson and Mr. Templar had to inform me, some days later, that I was not selected. However, I thoroughly enjoyed the experience and, I would like to think, learned another vital lesson about the game in the process. Having been chosen for that trial, it was amazing how many scouts suddenly started to turn up at games in which I was playing. Cliff Morgan, who followed my career closely, and was then chief scout at Bristol City, would appear at many of my matches. He would come and see me after the game, and offer me words of encouragement by saying either 'well done' or 'it won't be long until you're with us.' To be perfectly honest, from a very early age, the only team I wanted to play for was Bristol City. As a result, I couldn't believe it when Cliff Morgan asked if I would like to sign apprentice forms when I eventually left school. I was so happy that I signed without asking my parents' permission. It wasn't a particularly good move and they were not very pleased, to say the least. They wanted me to start an apprenticeship with a local business, Brecknol, Dolman and Rodgers, and train or play football in the evenings, as several other lads did at the time. My brother Martin had already started a very successful apprenticeship in north Bristol as a carpenter, but my heart was set, and my mind made up. I wanted to be a footballer and there was very little anyone could say or do to convince me otherwise. My eagerness to sign confirmed my naivety when it came to the professional game. I was so excited that the financial aspect and the small print didn't even enter the equation. It was only when a few players didn't sign immediately that my parents and I realised something wasn't right. The reason that the other lads hadn't signed was simple; a new rule was about to be introduced, whereby the club would have to pay the youngster a signing-on fee of £250. We were oblivious to the new ruling, and because of my haste, I never received the money. As far as I was concerned, the disappointment was short lived – I had signed for Bristol City, and money didn't even come into it.

At the time, I had no other firm offers (not that I wanted any), although Bristol Rovers were always coming along to matches to watch me play. Back then, of the twelve players in the Bristol Boys squad, it was a fairly regular occurrence to see nine of the lads going on to sign for City, with Rovers taking the remaining three. In my age group, Rovers picked up the likes of Larry Lloyd and Stuart Taylor, whilst John Mundy, Robert Williams and Dickie Down (despite being from the north of the city) joined me in signing for Bristol City.

On the Sunday after I had signed apprentice forms for City, I learned my first big lesson in football. As always, I intuitively decided to do it the hard way! In what had become a Sunday afternoon ritual, I walked over to Greville Smyth Park, for our usual kick-about. Although the faces changed every week, the usual names were there including Bobby Flicker, 'Rusty' Jacobs, John Rannahan, Phil and Brian Coggins, Steve Carey and my brother Martin, to name but a few. The notion of a 'friendly game' was one with which we never really got to grips. In one moment of over-exuberance, I went into a tackle with high hopes of football professionalism in the years ahead, only to come out of the collision with a broken right leg, and seemingly shattered dreams. As well as the obvious pain and look of disbelief on the faces of the lads around me, my thoughts went to the club, and the consequences of my actions. My fears were confirmed when the City manager, Fred Ford, went ballistic at the news. I knew I shouldn't have been playing outside of the club, even in a park game with my mates, but this made the reality all the more difficult to accept. The lure of a football, and my love of the game, had suddenly become one almighty obstacle to my realising my hopes and dreams. Fred Ford gave me the biggest telling off I had ever received in my life, but the club physiotherapist was a little more sympathetic. My only saving grace was that it was pre-season and that I had a couple of months until the start of the new campaign. The physio was hopeful that after six weeks I could get back into light training again, and fight for my place in the team before too many fixtures had passed. Needless to say, my Sunday afternoon kick-abouts with the lads stopped there!

As the playing side of football was now confined purely to playing for Bristol City, which of course was no problem, I looked for other hobbies. My enjoyment of snooker took me to a small snooker club in Ashton, on North Street, not far from where my mother worked for Wills. Some might say, including me, that it was a den of iniquity, with characters as dark as the bottom of the plaster on my right leg. Dave Sexton once said to me, 'if you're a good snooker player, then you've had a bit of a dodgy upbringing', which, judging by the way I played snooker meant my upbringing was never in question! The snooker club was called The Paragon and walking up the stairs into the darkness, for a fifteen-year-old, was a frightening and intimidating place to visit. Of the six tables, one, more often than not the match table, was being used for an underhand game of cards and for my own safety, I never asked any questions. As bleak a picture as I may paint now, it was a fun place to go. It was full of local characters such as 'Bill the Bad', who, even by 1964 standards was a few pounds overweight, and 'The Builder' who would make an entrance with pockets full of money offering to play anyone and everyone at snooker – for money of course. I often went to the Paragon two or three times a week, usually during the day, and there was always something going on in the background, whether it was hustling or illegal gambling. Inevitably, it resulted in people falling out, usually over cheating at cards or unpaid debts, but looking back, the experience was character building for me and, as a lad, relatively slight in build about to set out into the world of professional football, certainly didn't do me any harm.

What could have done me some harm was the time I had my pushbike stolen from outside The Paragon. I'm reluctant to tell the story even now, as I'm sure my mother still doesn't know. Mum, I'm sorry for what I am about to say. My parents gave me a new bike for Christmas and four days after Christmas Day 1964, I cycled to The Paragon for a game of snooker with the lads. We didn't have locks or chains and I left my bike outside. It sounds unbelievably stupid now, but everybody did it then and there usually wasn't a problem, but mine, being a new bike, must have seemed particularly appealing. When I came out to find that some little scally had nicked my new bike, I was absolutely dumbfounded as to what I should do. I panicked, but then realised a friend of mine had a bike similar, at least at a glance, to mine. I pleaded with him to let me 'borrow' his bike in the vain hope that my mother wouldn't realise mine was missing. Living in the flats, we used to keep the bikes in cages on the ground floor and as I suspected, from a distance, it looked remarkably like my own bike – a bit beaten up and nowhere near as shiny, but close enough. I believe I have got away with it until now – sorry Mum.

My first day as an apprentice at Bristol City Football Club was on 1 August 1964, a particularly memorable day, and a date I will never forget. There were twelve apprentices at the time, and I started with John Mundy, a lad with whom I had grown up and spent most of my footballing life. To mark the occasion, the Bristol *Evening Post* visited the B.O.C.M. ground on the Portway, where we were training, to take a photograph of us – jumping over the groundsman's wheelbarrow! We had signed a two-year contract with hopes of gaining a professional contract at the end of the period, at the age of seventeen. The days were spent mainly helping out around Ashton Gate, including cleaning and painting the terraces and changing rooms, as well as cleaning boots. If we were lucky, we would then train in the afternoon, learning the trade that we all wanted to adopt so desperately. We had a fantastic youth squad at the time – John Macey, Trevor Jacobs, David Down, Trevor Tainton, Graham Tanner, John Giles and Danny

Bartley were just a few of the players with whom I had to compete to win a place in the youth team. Most of these lads had a year's age and experience advantage over me (many being second-year apprentices), but I was determined to prove myself. I found it extremely hard initially, mainly because we weren't training very much at all. We were kept so busy carrying out our chores around the ground that our time with a football was kept at a minimum. As a result I found it difficult to compete with the bigger lads who had already started to see the benefit of a whole year's training. In saying that, after several months of 'full-time training', I began to get stronger, and show the potential I had promised in the years before.

In addition to 'chores' at the ground, another of my tasks involved visiting the local bookmakers – either the one by the Rising Sun pub along from Ashton Gate, or one of the two on North Street. Usually I was putting the bets on for 'Dickie' Down and Johnny Giles even though I wasn't old enough to bet myself! They knew I wasn't old enough to bet, but it didn't stop me trying, or them accepting my wager. Almost straightaway I invariably had a bet myself, as well as placing the other players' bets. The introduction of the 4-3-3 and 4-4-2 formations around this time was almost alien to me after years as an 'inside forward'. The only system I really knew then was a 6-4-1, more commonly known as a Yankee – six doubles, four trebles and an accumulator – and that was the closest I had come to a 4-3-3! Little did I know at the time that it would do me no favours in the thirty years that followed. Early on in my betting, I remember placing a sixpence-place-accumulator for all the trap six greyhounds in every race at Hackney one Saturday – meaning that the trap six greyhound had to finish in the first two in each of the ten races that afternoon. Would you believe it, they all did as well! I won about £90 that day, which was a lot of money then. I told my mum and gave her a share of the winnings, but it was big wins like that early on that got me hooked, and would ultimately lead me down the wrong path in the years ahead.

I continued to work hard at my game, and improved enough to win a place in the youth team. It was only ten months after I had signed as an apprentice that I was a regular in the line-up.

I was happy just to be playing football for a living, but we certainly didn't do it for the money. I was earning £5 a week, and out of that, Fred Ford ensured that we saved some money each week – this was kept at the club for us, and was there for us should we ever have needed it. I also gave my mum housekeeping money, and at the end of it all, I would be left with about £1.50 for myself. It doesn't sound a lot today, but it seemed to go a fair way in the mid-sixties. We were very limited even then, as to what we could and couldn't get up to. More often than not, it would be a trip to the pictures, and I would never drink lager, it was always lemonade or cola back then! The dress code at the club was very strict, and we always wore a shirt and tie to games. I give credit to my parents for spending the money to give me smart attire in the early days, and I was always proud of my appearance. As an aspiring sixteen-year-old footballer, it was very important to get into good habits and make an impression when travelling to the likes of Plymouth Argyle. It was a great time for me off the pitch as well as on it, with the influence of music playing a big part in my life. In particular, I loved soul and Motown music and artists such as Stevie Wonder, Diana Ross and The Four Tops, some of whom we could see live in and around Bristol. It was generally a time of great musical and sociological change, as Britain had been invaded by the 'Mods' and 'Rockers'. Despite my passion for music and good clothes, I resisted the urge to get involved. Football was my one love, and, as a result, music and girls were still very much second-best in my eyes. However, when I was playing for the youth team at Ashton Gate, many of the local school girls would turn up at the ground, and also at the nearby Robins Café where we would often take our breaks. In fact, I'd be lying if I didn't say we used to wait in the friendly family-run café for the girls from Ashton Park School to come in on some days. It was the time of the mini-skirt, and as impressionable teenagers, we liked nothing better than attention from the opposite sex. Little did I know at the time, that my future wife, Trish, would be from this group of schoolgirls.

One friend of mine at the time was Wally Watkins, who played for both City and Rovers but was some two or three years older than me, but I think my mother thought he was going to lead me astray. Wally, along with Paul Mizon and Steve Carey, was out most nights enjoying himself, but being a footballer, dedication and staying in a few nights during the week was the difference between possible success and a wasted talent. Being released after two years would be absolutely no use to me, I wanted to be a professional footballer and that was that!

I owe a tremendous amount to my parents, not least for the way they looked after me, and helped me develop between the somewhat awkward ages of fifteen and seventeen. Their concern for me was obvious; if I didn't make it into the professional ranks, they were worried that I would be finished, and left on the scrapheap with so many other lads, with no further education or a trade behind me. I was incredibly lucky that my parents weren't overly strict, and had the flexibility to allow me to fulfil my dreams. In saying that, my father always gave me a curfew to be home in the evenings (usually around eleven o'clock) – and this simply was not up for discussion! Although it did seem a hindrance at the time, it was for the best in terms of my future career. Usually, I would only be visiting one of the many picture houses in Bristol at the time. These included the Odeon in Union Street, or the Gaumont in Baldwin Street in the centre of town; or the Rex in North Street, Bedminster. If my father had allowed me to stroll in at three in the morning, who knows what mischief I'd have got up to, not to mention ruining my chances at City.

Martin played his football for a well-known local Bristol Suburban League team called Exeter United. Their home pitch was in the park opposite Ashton Gate, but the social side of the club was just as important as the football itself. I always remember Martin coming home from his work as a carpenter and dashing out most nights during the week, as well as at the weekend. If it wasn't a football match or training with the lads, it was to play darts or skittles. When the sport was over they would simply meet up at the Rising Sun on Ashton Road, and spend hours on end putting the world to rights over a few pints, before getting fish and chips in the shop next door on the way home. I enjoyed nothing more than stopping and sitting on the wall of Ashton Park on a Saturday lunchtime to watch the lads play in their famous gold-and-black strip before I went over to Ashton Gate. I wasn't the only one either, as whenever City were playing at home, Exeter United would get nearly half the crowd watching them in the park as the pre-match entertainment. You were always guaranteed a laugh, even moments of brilliance that wouldn't have looked out of place across the road, but more often than not you'd get to witness a punch-up. Exeter United had a tremendous bunch of lads, not to mention a great sense of spirit and camaraderie, and this would continue for decades to come.

To say Martin was injury-prone would be a little unfair, but he always seemed to be in plaster. The first occasion was whilst he was on scout camp at Exmouth. The family received a telephone call to say he had fallen out of a tree and broken his leg, which sounded typical of Martin. He also broke his leg two or three times playing football, as well as an arm and his nose, but this didn't stop him making over three hundred appearances for Exeter United at centre-half. Needless to say, he did get his own back on a few of the lads that crocked him over the years, which earned him the nickname 'Clogger Garland'!

It was towards the end of my first year as an apprentice at City that I missed the last bus home from Old Market, in the centre of Bristol, after a night out. I didn't have enough money for a taxi, so in a desperate attempt to get home in time to make my dad's curfew, I ran the three miles or so through the Redcliffe area, into Bedminster, and finally home to Ashton. Unluckily for me, my dad was waiting for me when I walked through the door. I was sweating like a pig, not only because I had run a fair way, but also in anticipation of his reaction. He thought I had been out fighting and as he didn't believe my story, we went to bed that night on a big argument. My actions the next day, I have lived to regret immensely ever since. I packed a bag early, and went straight over to Ashton Gate. I asked for the money that I had been saving in my account under Fred Ford's scheme and set off for Weymouth alone on the train. It left my parents at home feeling miserable, and I was away for seven or eight days during the season, which put everything I had ever cared about - my family and football – in jeopardy. Teenagers do this sort of thing, and parents have to put up with a lot, but my actions were inexcusable. I chose Weymouth because this was where my parents used to take me on holiday, and I knew the place reasonably well. We also had relations living not too far away in Portland Bill.

I checked into a bed-and-breakfast as soon as I arrived. I'm sure the lady was a little dubious that a young lad had turned up from Bristol with a bag and not a lot else, but she let me stay nevertheless. My lasting memory of this trip was of sitting in amusement arcades for hours on end playing bingo. When I eventually ran out of money one week later, I had to hitch-hike home, as I didn't even save enough money for the return journey. I didn't realise how hard hitch-hiking was going to be and ended up walking from Weymouth to Dorchester before I got a lift. I knew what a stupid fool I had been and regretted all the heartache I had caused my mother and father. I can only hope that I made up for the errors of my ways in the years ahead, and that this was just a blip on my teenage record. Back at Ashton Gate, Mr Ford was waiting to greet me. I was expecting the worst, but he was very good about it. He did say that he should've given me 'a clip round the ear', but just told me to get on and concentrate on my football – to be given that second chance at the club I loved was something for which I would be eternally grateful!

I trained harder than ever before, and the team was playing well. We were playing in the Wessex Youth League, and visited Cardiff City, Swindon Town, Swansea City and Bristol Rovers amongst others. Playing against Bristol Rovers even at that level meant a fiercely competitive fixture and great rivalry, as we came up against schoolboy friends and the likes of Larry Lloyd, Stuart Taylor, Glyn Jones and Bobby Brown. In the two years I played in the Wessex Youth League, I never lost against Rovers, a record of which I was particularly proud.

As I moved into my second year as an apprentice, after winning the league and scoring my fair share of goals along the way, I realised I was entering the most important twelve months of my life. At the pre-season photo-shoot, I was selected to stand next to my hero John Atyeo. The club hoped that the youngsters selected to stand alongside the first-team regulars would follow in their footsteps, which gave me a massive boost. Thoughts started to go through my mind, and I wondered whether, if I worked hard at my game, I could reach the same heights, or even a small part of what 'Big John' achieved. One of the highlights of the second year was the visit of the England Youth team to Ashton Gate to play us in a friendly on Tuesday, 8 February 1966. England manager Alf Ramsey sat in the cold stand to watch the game, unaware as to exactly what would happen in the months ahead, which would give him a special place in the country's history. Nearly 5,000 turned up to watch the game in terrible conditions, including my new girlfriend Trish (it didn't take long for my attitude towards girls to change), and despite losing 5-0, it was a fantastic experience. Even though we were comprehensively out-played, I was chosen to join the England training party at Lilleshall shortly afterwards and as a result played in a warm-up game for England Youth against Crystal Palace Under-20s at Selhurst Park later that year. I came on at half-time and had few opportunities to score, but even with Peter Shilton between the sticks for us, we lost 1-0. I also played one other game, against

Queens Park Rangers Under-20s, which was a tremendous experience not only for the match itself on Monday, but because we went to watch the full England team play against Czechoslovakia at Wembley two days later, before returning to Bristol the following day. These experiences were particular high points in my career. Pulling on the England shirt, even in warm-up games, and looking down to see the 'Three Lions' was unbelievable, and made me feel ten feet tall. Looking back to my school days, I never envisaged putting on a Bristol City shirt, let alone an England jersey, and I had achieved both within two years of leaving school. It was all beyond my wildest dreams.

Following another successful season with Bristol City's youth team, during which we won the Wessex Youth League (for a third consecutive season), and in which I also had outings for the reserve team, I was called into Fred Ford's office on 29 April 1966, five days after my seventeenth birthday. He offered me a full-time professional contract, which really was my dream come true. The report and photograph in the following day's Bristol *Evening Post* confirmed my new professional status.

Despite having the extra pressure of being regarded as 'one of the most exciting discoveries in Bristol for years', I was happy to live up to the billing, and the accolade did wonders for my confidence. All I can remember about signing was that negotiations on my salary were very swift and sweet. Fred Ford offered me £15 a week and said 'take it or leave it' – I told him to give me the pen and I signed immediately, there was no negotiating that! The feeling of signing that contract was something else, and even though the money was secondary, a £10 a week rise was the icing on the cake. Later on, I spoke to Gordon Parr, a senior professional in whom I often confided. He gave me one or two pieces of information, and I learned that some of the senior professionals were on nowhere near £15 a week, so I was thankful that, on this occasion, I kept my mouth shut and just signed.

I was still naïve when it came to financial negotiations in football, but, in 1966, the clubs at the top level were still very much in control, unlike today, where the players appear to call all the shots. The first thing I did after Mr Ford's offer was to run home to my mother and father and tell them the news. They were over the moon, and more importantly, it gave me the opportunity to prove that I hadn't let them down.

As I achieved one major goal in my life, so I set myself new targets. I looked forward to my first season as a professional footballer immensely, and my objective for the year ahead, and the years that followed, was clear – to break into the Bristol City first team…and stay there!

CHAPTER TWO

MAKING IT

Pre-season training had gone well, made easier by the fact that I had kept myself fit during the summer months in readiness for the new season and the challenges that lay ahead. As a youngster, new to the professional ranks, playing in any game seemed a bonus. I was as enthusiastic and hard-working as ever and eager to learn, but I was also in touch with the reality that owing to my age, size and the players around me, continuing to play games in the reserves – let alone break into the first-team – would be tough. Thankfully I didn't have to wait long for another chance in the reserves. I played well in the pre-season fixtures and also managed to score a few goals, which helped with my own confidence. I felt I had earned my place in the reserve team as the new season approached.

I continued to play well for City's second string and was happy with the way my career was progressing, when a bolt out of the blue hit me one day in mid-November. Bristol City were due to play a first-team friendly against a German outfit called Hannover 96 for 'The Friendship Cup'. It would be the first game in what it was hoped would become an annual fixture between City and Hannover, who were one of the big shots in the then German Super League. Harry Dolman boldly predicted in the media beforehand that City would be the first holders of the cup, but unfortunately wasn't present to witness the whole match that he had been instrumental in organising. He had been taken ill the day before and despite getting up from his sick bed to attend the match, he left Ashton Gate at half-time with the score at 1–1. I realised the significance of this match for me only the day before, when Fred Ford called me into his office to say I would be in the first-team squad. What he forgot to tell me was not only would I be in the squad, but that I would actually be starting the match. The next day, on Wednesday, 16 November 1966, I made my first-team debut for Bristol City Football Club at the age of seventeen-and-a-half-years-old. I was the youngest player for seven years to make their debut, the youngest since Jantzen Derrick. This was a particular honour for me, as Jantzen was a great hero of mine and one hell of a player! The Hannover side had three German internationals, including striker Walter Rodekamp who had played against England in Nuremberg the year before. On this occasion, he scored one and set up another in a 3–2 win for Hannover. I remember the City fans getting angered by the German style of play – often audacious and casual at the back, but always with an air of organised assurance. I had few chances to shine during the game and although I was pleased with my overall contribution, was replaced in the second half by Terry Bush. Even though I played just over one half, the experience of pulling on the first-team's red jersey (there is a difference, even if it is only psychological) and playing with the first-team players was fantastic. I remember the one thing constantly going through my mind during my time on the pitch, on the bench and when I lay in bed that night was 'I can't wait to make my league debut'.

In the run-up to the Hannover game, my physical attributes were described, as usual, in the local press. I failed to see how me being slim and fair-haired had any bearing on my overall ability. Nevertheless, it was something that would appear in pretty much every article about me. In addition, local journalists also saw me as 'one of the brightest prospects on City's staff…with an abundance of skill, class and potential', which certainly gave my confidence a huge boost. Despite those nice words, there really was only one man I had to impress – Fred Ford. Physically, I had grown about six inches in the last year, which could only benefit my case to break into the first-team if thought good enough. However, Mr Ford was quoted in the press leading up to my debut as saying 'Chris lacks strength and isn't ready for the first-team just yet'. In my own mind I wasn't sure if I had done enough during the match to convince him otherwise. I was still scoring regularly for the youth team and reserves, hitting all four goals against Street in a 4–0 Somerset Professional Cup tie and twice in two games against Bristol Rovers in the space of a week – maintaining my own unbeaten record at all levels against our biggest rivals. In the back of my mind I wondered if I had begun to fulfil just a small part of the potential that the media had been talking about for so long. The local press in particular began to champion me and two weeks after my initial introduction to life in the first team, Mr Ford pulled me to one side in training. With a protective hand on my shoulder, he said, 'You've been selected to play for the first-team tomorrow against Preston North End.' Exactly what else he said to me is a blur. I couldn't hide the broad smile across my face and I just wanted to shout out to the flats opposite and scream so my mother could hear me. Remembering my new-found professionalism, I resisted the urge, which was probably just as well because my mother wouldn't have heard me, not least because she was at work about half-a-mile away! The first thing I did after training was rush home to tell Mum (my father was still at work) that I was going to play in the first-team the next day and that one of my first-ever dreams was about to be fulfilled.

My parents had watched me play week-in-week-out since the beginning. Right from when my mother watched me play in all weathers at the Clanage for South Street Primary School, through to Bristol Boys and Bristol City Youth Team. Despite knowing that they would never be anything other than supportive, at City, if I knew my parents were watching in the stand at Ashton Gate, I became incredibly nervous. I didn't like them watching me. There was no particular reason for this and I often felt guilty, but thankfully both my parents understood and accommodated my wishes. As a result, they watched my debut the following day from home, overlooking Ashton Gate from the sixth floor in Winterstoke House flats, with probably a better view of the game than anybody else in the 10,815 crowd inside the ground.

On the day of the match I received numerous good-luck wishes and cards from friends, family and staff at Ashton Gate and I knew that Saturday, 3 December 1966 would be a date that stuck in my mind for a long time. I was to replace the highly-thought-of and leading scorer Gerry Sharpe, who had a throat infection. This added to the pressure, but it was only really when I walked into the changing room that the reality kicked in. Unfortunately, manager Fred Ford wasn't there to witness my debut. He decided to go to another game and have a look at signing another forward. It did disappoint me initially, but I knew that with a good performance, I could prove my value to the players and staff who *were* at the match. I was also under no illusion that Mr. Ford would have requested a full report on my display on his return. The City line-up included many of the stars I had admired and looked up to over the years as well as a few that I had grown up around. The starting line-up was: Mike Gibson, Tony Ford, Alec Briggs, Chuck Drury, Jack Connor, Gordon Low, Ray Savino, myself, Terry Bush, John Quigley and Danny Bartley. All the players were supportive, but a few of the senior players like Jack Connor, Gordon Low and John Quigley realised my excited but apprehensive front in Mr Ford's absence. They passed on words of advice, assuring me everything would be fine, to play my own game as I had done for the last eighteen months and to enjoy it. Howard Kendall, who went on to have a very successful managerial career, was also a highly rated wing-half for Preston and was billed in the press to mark me for much of the game. My mind was so focussed on the game and doing myself justice that I didn't really take in the atmosphere, I just knew that I loved the experience. The first half was largely one-sided in Preston's favour, but one moment of indecisiveness in the Preston midfield gave me my opportunity to change the course of the game. I found the ball at my feet and ran towards Alan Kelly in the Preston goal. I spotted Chuck Drury dart inside and found him with a pass, which he in turn guided to John Quigley. John waited for Kelly to commit and hit a shot into the corner out of the keeper's reach. I guess it was against the run of play, but to be quite honest I couldn't have cared less, we were one-nil up on my debut. Terry Bush sealed the points in the second half with a cracking 40-yard strike from the touchline, which sent a timely reminder to the absent Fred Ford, who potentially was watching Terry's successor in City's strike force. We won the match 2–0 and despite not scoring, I was happy with my performance and setting up the first goal. My team-mates were also complimentary about my display and I felt sure that I would only benefit from my first experience of Second Division football. After the high of playing and the euphoria of the day, little did I know at the time that my debut against Preston would be my only first-team appearance that season.

After what was considered a decent first showing for the first-team by players, supporters and the media, it was extremely disappointing and frustrating – even as a seventeen year-old – to be left out of the squad for the next game. With the team struggling at the bottom of the Second Division, Fred Ford decided to opt for experience to get the club out of trouble. Even though I continued to play well and score regularly for the reserves, I felt that I was being overlooked, with the first-team struggling to get results. In the years that followed, I spoke to Fred when he was coaching at Oxford United and he said he felt he needed to protect me at the time. Not only did he want to shelter me from the numerous 'cloggers' in the division, who were more than capable of breaking a bright young player's leg, but he also wanted to protect my confidence. He feared that my own self-belief would have been damaged by any backlash from media or fans because of the club's poor performances. At the time, I wondered if my mother's words about football being a precarious profession for a teenager would come back to haunt me and also if, or indeed when, my opportunity would come. It would be over nine months before I would get my second chance at first-team football.

After escaping relegation in the 1966–67 season by finishing in 15th position – a creditable conclusion given our early season form – it was vital that a good start was made to the new campaign. Our top scorer that season was Roger 'Lou' Peters with a far-from-healthy nine league goals and consequently hitting the back of the net more often had become every player's responsibility. After another seemingly positive pre-season, my appearances were still strictly limited to the reserves, despite my continuing to score on a regular basis. I did receive an award early on in the season, but unfortunately it had little to do with my footballing prowess. I was named top in the Football League's review of the Top Ten 'handsome players'. It caused a bit of a stir in the local press, and whilst I obviously agreed wholeheartedly with the judges, one young lady certainly didn't. It upset her so much that she felt the need to write to the Bristol *Evening Post*: '...I strongly disagree with this and think that Wayne Jones of Bristol Rovers is much more handsome.' Living in Filton, north Bristol, it was quite clear that her loyalties were safely in sight of the Bristol Gas Works. She even concluded her letter by asking for support in setting up a petition! As far as I'm concerned, the term 'Gas Head', now widely used when referring to followers of Bristol Rovers, could well have started as a result of that somewhat delirious letter. I mean, Wayne Jones?

Although it is always nice to receive the attention and tongue-in-cheek awards like that, I was happy in my first 'serious' relationship with Trish, which was now into its second year. In addition, all my efforts were being thrown into gaining that elusive second appearance for the first eleven. The 1967–68 season, once again, started slowly for the first-team, losing six and drawing one out of their first eight fixtures. This included two 5–0 defeats, one against Ipswich Town in the league and the other at the hands of Everton in the League Cup. Manager Fred Ford was feeling the pressure and many people felt that City's home fixture against Blackpool on 16 September could well be his final opportunity to turn things around. Once again I was left out of the squad, along with several other promising youngsters, and City crashed to a 4–2 loss. Sure enough, as many predicted, Fred Ford was sacked after the match, leaving trainer and physio, Les Bardsley, as temporary manager. Les was certainly no stranger to the caretaker manager role, having taken the reins following the previous departures of Pat Beasley in 1958 and Peter Doherty in 1960. On this occasion, Les and the team would have another true test of physical and mental toughness at The Den, home of Millwall. Little did I know at the time that I would be part of the examination that would analyse the strength and depth of the club's resources as we moved into a new era at Ashton Gate.

The sports pages of the local press were full of the sacking of Fred Ford and, whilst most corners of the media agreed with the decision, they were equally as preoccupied with the speculation as to who would be his successor. For now at least Les Bardsley was in charge and on the Wednesday before the Millwall match, he stirred up the reporters once again when he announced the changes in personnel for the game. Club captain Gordon Low and his wing-half partner Gordon Parr were both dropped from the line-up. Five changes were made, two of which were positional, with Johnny Quigley moving to right-half and winger Jantzen Derrick moved inside. In addition, Terry Bush was recalled and Dickie Down and myself were given 'shock' call-ups. Dickie, now nineteen, had scored five times in eight appearances last season, but similarly to me, had struggled to break into Fred Ford's side this term, making just one substitute appearance. I had waited almost a year for this opportunity and even as an eighteen year-old heading into the hostility of The Den, I was determined to take it with both hands.

The Den always was a frightening place to visit. Even as you walked around the pitch before the game, there was a distinct possibility that someone would feel the need to spit and swear at you. What was meant to be a relaxed pre-match look at the pitch, often turned into a major clean-up operation in the dressing room after, as you tried to remove some idiot's welcome off the shoulder and back of your blazer. The Millwall fans had their favourites on the pitch and the players would always play up to it – very few teams went there and actually got a result. As we expected, the game itself was a battle and we played out a hard-fought 1–1 draw, thanks to a fantastic strike from Chris Crowe in the 23rd minute. Unfortunately our lead lasted only seven minutes, but the performance overall and spirit in the dressing room was one of optimism and renewed hope. I managed to get off the pitch in one piece, but at Millwall you didn't walk off the pitch, you ran off! I really didn't think crowds were like that any more, because everywhere else you played, you were applauded if you did something good. Not here – if you got any kind of result in your favour, you simply didn't hang about! Chairman Harry Dolman joined us, as usual, on the team coach after the game and he was beaming from ear-to-ear as he stopped and spoke to each player as he made his way down the bus. I was particularly pleased for Les Bardsley, who not only took a risk in changing to a 4-2-4 formation, but also, at the risk of being unpopular, gave Dickie and me another chance. I was happy with my own performance and at the same time, was pleased with one particular review by Peter Godsiff in the Bristol *Evening Post*. He wrote, 'Garland was the more impressive of the youngsters thrust into the attack and showed enough potential to remain a first-team player.' I hoped and prayed he was right!

I walked the short distance into training on the Monday morning and before I could get changed into my training kit, Les called me into his office to say I would be retaining my place for the following Saturday's fixture against Hull City. This was highly unusual and different to anything I had experienced before as you still had a week's training to prove yourself. Nevertheless, I wasn't about to complain and I was delighted that Peter Godsiff's crystal ball hadn't let him down on this occasion. This would be one of the major turning points in my career. We drew 3–3 with Hull City at Ashton Gate and after we'd gone a goal down within a minute, I equalised, scoring my first league goal for City just two minutes later. In addition, I grabbed the headlines in the Monday papers, being billed as 'the blond, eighteen-year-old hero', but it was really the outstanding performance of Chris Crowe that helped to get us the point we deserved. That evening after the match, I felt, to some extent at least, I had finally arrived. The crowds seemed to favour me, being the local lad. Back then, with the exception of one or two players like Gordon Parr, there were very few Bristolians at Bristol City. There's no doubt that over the years, the supporters at Ashton Gate really have liked a local lad pulling on the red shirt and today is certainly no different.

After remaining undefeated whilst in charge and gaining two vital points that we so desperately needed, Les Bardsley would once again stand down as caretaker manager. Bristol City announced they were to appoint a new, young manager by the name of Alan Dicks, who was then assistant manager to Jimmy Hill at Coventry City. Alan would be in the stand to watch our fixture with Crystal Palace at Selhurst Park the following Saturday. In what would be Les Bardsley's final match at the helm, he included me in the starting line-up again, for my third consecutive match in the first-team. Palace were currently top-of-the-table and it wouldn't have been many of the players' choice of match to impress a new boss in front of a 20,000 strong really partisan crowd. However, for an hour of the game we more than matched them, with chances at either end and Mike Gibson in the City goal pulling off a number of fine saves. It was only after 63 minutes that Steve Kember, who I had played against nearly four years previously in the English FA trial at Ilford, scored the first of Palace's two goals. Once again, the press were positive about the performance of the team despite the reverse and were also complimentary about my own showing. The unknown factor from all the players' perspective was how Alan Dicks had perceived the collective and individual perform-ances from the stand. As predicted, Alan was confirmed as the new manager of Bristol City Football Club on Monday, 9 October 1967 and his first game in charge would be the local derby fixture against Cardiff City at Ashton Gate.

Two days before the Cardiff game, Alan called me into his office to discuss the forthcoming fixture. To my disappointment, he told me that he would be relying on experienced players to help get City out of trouble at the foot of the Second Division and that I would not be playing on Saturday. Clearly the name of the game was 'experienced players' and younger players found it extremely difficult to break into the senior side to prove their value. Fred Ford and now Alan Dicks advocated similar philosophies when the team was struggling, but I honestly felt that, on this occasion, I had earned my place in the first-team starting line-up regardless of age and experience. Alan said he was impressed with my performance at Crystal Palace and if the players selected did not perform, I would be straight back in the side. At the time it was scant consolation, but on the Saturday, City drew

1–1 and sure enough, Alan was true to his word. I replaced Danny Bartley in a forward-line reshuffle for the game against Portsmouth at Fratton Park. We went on to lose two-nil in a very poor game with little incident. Unfortunately, for me, the game ended prematurely, as I retired injured shortly before half-time with a badly bruised thigh. I had some goal-scoring chances before I went off and created a couple more for the team, but it seemed to be one of those days when we could have played all night and still not hit the back of the net. Despite the injury, which I recovered from to make training on the Monday, and the missed chances, I really didn't look back after that game. Although Alan Dicks had left me out of the side for his first match in charge, I was a regular for the rest of the 1967–68 season. I played thirty-two league and cup games and scored nine goals – equalling the total scored by Lou Peters the previous season. It doesn't sound a fantastic record now, but at the age of eighteen, I was more than pleased with my tally. Every goal was important and I scored some vital goals along the way, as the club continued to struggle at the bottom of Division Two. We eventually finished in nineteenth position, just avoiding the drop, but I dread to think what would have happened if Alan Dicks hadn't pulled his first masterstroke since arriving at Ashton Gate. My tally of nine goals may have matched last season's leading hit-man, but it was still some way off this campaign's top marksman – John Galley. Scoring goals was a major problem at City and Alan Dicks recognised this immediately. Two months after taking charge, he finally got his man. John was signed for £25,000 from Rotherham United in December 1967 and scored sixteen league and two FA Cup goals in twenty-six appearances. This included a debut to remember, when he scored all three goals in a three-nil away win at Huddersfield, a performance that elevated him to hero status instantly with the supporters. As well as being a fantastic acquisition for the team, one week before Christmas, this was the best present I could have asked for. My height and size had always been reported on in the media as I was just over 5'10", but looking back at some of my hair cuts, there's no doubt that I was touching six-foot at some points in my career! Nevertheless, in 1967, I was crying out for a centre-forward to play off – someone very much in the mould of the legendary John Atyeo. In John Galley, at 6'3", I had my dream ally in the City front-line and we struck up a good partnership from day one. He was big, strong, fantastic in the air and certainly knew where the goal was. We had a great understanding; John would win everything in the air and I would be buzzing around feeding off his knock-ons and knock-downs. I learnt a lot from John, as I did with Johnny Quigley, who was one of the best midfielders I have played with or against. While he may have not been the quickest of players, he had great movement and was a terrific passer of the ball who was always looking for little one-twos. He lived for the game and was a great man to know both on and off the field. Sadly, he has since passed away.

With the arrival of John Galley, the whole mood around Ashton Gate changed and in addition to improved fortunes in the league, we also embarked on a decent run in the FA Cup. As I eagerly awaited the Third Round draw for the first time as a regular first-team player, I couldn't believe my ears when I heard, 'Bristol City...will play...Bristol Rovers.' At the first time of asking, a bumper crowd of 37,000 packed into Ashton Gate to witness a disappointing, and largely uneventful, 0–0 draw. The replay quickly followed at Eastville, where another great crowd of 36,000 squeezed in. I think the Rovers boys thought they would take us back to Eastville and give us a pounding, but we beat them 2–1 and I, once again, continued my unbeaten record against them. To be fair, the atmosphere on Derby Day was amazing and although I wasn't particularly fond of the place, Eastville was certainly no different. I remember the coach driving along Stapleton Road and past Eastville Park on the way to the game and it was incredible to see the thousands of fans and the keen look of anticipation on their faces. It really sent it home to you how much the fixture meant to the people of Bristol – not that I needed any telling! As a boy I remembered being marched by the police, along with thousands of other City fans, through the roads leading to Eastville. The excitement I felt then was no different to what the fans felt on this day, or come to that, what I was still feeling as a player. The Gloucester Cup games between City and Rovers often created more problems and intense passion between players and fans than a lot of the league fixtures. Although a 'friendly-match', a couple of weeks before the so-say serious stuff began, it often became an annual fixture of high importance and great local pride, as City and Rovers were usually in different divisions. On top of the match itself, you won gold medals and for many of the players, it was *the* game to look forward to. Only if we were drawn together in cup competitions could we do battle in a 'competitive' arena. The term 'friendly-match' could

probably have not been more inappropriately used. Owing to the
rarity of the occasion, it was particularly nice to beat them in the FA
Cup, but in the Fourth Round we were given another tricky tie against
Middlesbrough. Nearly 30,000 turned up to watch, but once again the
first match ended all square at 1–1, after I had equalised for City
shortly before half-time. Despite going a goal down after only eight
minutes, we showed the new-found belief in ourselves and could have
clinched the tie at Ayresome Park had it not been for the
Middlesbrough keeper, Willie Whigham, making a string of fine
saves. Nevertheless, we took Boro back to Ashton Gate and subsequently beat them by the same score that defeated Bristol Rovers. The
2–1 score-line certainly didn't flatter us and the goals by Jack Connor
and John Galley could have, and should have, been added to. Once
again despite being transfer-listed, Jantzen Derrick turned in a typical
match-winning performance full of skill and trickery, masterminding
many of City's attacks and giving the Boro full-back a torrid time. All
of a sudden, we were in the Fifth Round of the FA Cup and the
Evening Post's headline – 'A GLITTERING PRIZE FOR CITY' –
couldn't have been more suitable. We had been drawn away to Leeds
United, certainly one of the best teams in the country and full of
household names, many of whom I had admired as a schoolboy.

Shortly before leaving Ashton Gate, we had a photo-call in our suits
in the car park in front of the Grand Stand. Admittedly it wasn't one
of my better pictures, as we were looking straight into the bright
sunshine and I had my eyes shut. I remember the journey to Leeds
being quieter than normal. This was one of the biggest games of my
career so far, but this was also the case for many players in the squad.
A crowd of over 45,000 packed into Elland Road to watch the Fifth
Round tie, but unfortunately the game would be remembered for the
wrong reasons. Bad tackles, bookings and personal feuds all over the
pitch spoilt what should have been a fantastic spectacle. I'm still not
sure why, maybe we were all wound up as the underdogs and Leeds
thought they could just stroll past us with likes of Billy Bremner,
Norman Hunter and John Giles. After all, this was the same Leeds
United side that took the piss out of Southampton that time with all
the fancy flicks and passes and as far as they were concerned, Bristol
City was a team they should be stuffing four or five-nil. Things
weren't going the way the Leeds lads were hoping and eventually in
the early stages of the second half, every individual tussle reached

boiling point. Leeds had scored their second goal of the game seconds before half-time, but despite having this comfort zone came out literally kicking and fighting in the second period. City were by no means blameless and one reporter was quoted as saying that 'both sides had their own Peter O'Toole' because of the amount of feigning and dramatic falls that were occurring all over the pitch. Things really 'kicked off' when Peter Lorimer went past John Quigley who grabbed Lorimer's leg in an attempt to stop him. Lorimer kicked out and caught John in the chest. Peter was booked for his troubles and then I followed him into the referee's book shortly after for kicking Billy Bremner from behind. It was a stupid way to get booked, but by the standards set by some tackles was also fairly innocuous. The referee, Mr Dimond, had tried to let play flow where possible, but as a result had gradually lost control of the game. Whilst the referee was concentrating on spelling my name correctly, Lorimer threw the ball with some venom at Gerry Sharpe's head, knocking him to the floor. Les Bardsley came on to give Gerry treatment and the ref commented to Les that 'he needed eyes in the back of his head for this game'. I wished he had as well. While all this was going on, Gary Sprake, the Leeds' keeper was obviously feeling left out of matters and had one of his many mad moments. With my back turned, he walked up to me and threw a punch which caught me square on the jaw, splitting my lip and sending me crashing to inspect the turf at closer quarters. With all that was going on, Mr Dimond missed the punch, but thankfully an eagle-eyed linesman saw everything. Peter Lorimer took the green jersey as Sprake was promptly sent off with a look of disbelief on his face. I recovered to finish the last twenty minutes of the match, but Sprake would miss three vital matches in five days through suspension, one of which was Leeds' Fairs Cup Quarter-Final 2nd Leg against Rangers. It was some justice at least, because this game left a really bad taste in my mouth for years to come. It was a real shame, because whilst Leeds United had some very skilful players, they also had one or two individuals who would be completely out of order at times. Nevertheless, despite Leeds being down to ten men, we couldn't break down a resolute defence and eventually lost the match two-nil. The season ended for me personally with speculation in the local and national press, with rumours about Tottenham Hotspur and a whole host of other top-flight clubs being interested in signing me. It was certainly nice to get the attention from big clubs and big-name managers like Bill Nicholson and Tommy Docherty, then of Aston Villa, but I was more than happy playing my football at Bristol City. Alan Dicks was quoted in the media as saying, 'We shall not sell Garland for two years unless our financial position makes it impossible to keep him.' I was regularly reported as valued in the £100,000 bracket, which for a nineteen-year-old, would have been a major financial risk for any club in the country.

After the events of the 67–68 season and establishing myself as a first-team regular, it was up to me to keep putting in the work and the performances into the new term. The speculation about my future continued, with seemingly a new club every week entering the equation. Stoke City and West Bromwich Albion were the latest clubs to show an interest, but my focus was on the season ahead at Ashton Gate. One match that stands out early on from the 1968–69 season was against Derby County. I was playing against the great Dave Mackay and felt as though I definitely got the better of him on this particular day. He came up to me at the end of the game, shook my hand and said, 'You'll have a great career in football if you carry on playing like you did today.' For Dave Mackay at his peak to say that was one of the biggest compliments I could have received. He was an unbelievable player. Dave had a reputation for being a hard player, which I would certainly endorse, but he was never dirty. He had great upper-body strength and nine times out of ten would come out from a tackle with the ball. Anyone can go over the top of a ball, but that's not being hard, that's just being bloody stupid and Dave just wasn't that kind of player. I should have made the most of that occasion as I rarely got any joy the times I played against him in numerous subsequent matches.

The worst tackle I have ever seen in football was on one of my own team mates. Gerry Sharpe, as I have mentioned previously, was a young and very talented footballer. In the January of 1971, City played Middlesbrough at Ashton Gate. With City two-nil up and only a few minutes to go, a short lad by the name of McMordie went over the top of the ball and left Gerry in a heap on the turf. It was so bad that Gerry's bone was sticking out through his leg, which he very nearly lost in hospital, as the line markings had infected the wound. I was close to the incident and felt physically sick, whilst Gordon Parr went absolutely berserk as McMordie, who didn't bat an eyelid, wasn't even sent off. I remember that later on the same year, City went on an end-of-season trip to Spain, and Middlesbrough were staying in the same resort. A few of the players like Gordon Parr wanted to go and sort him out, but that would have only made things worse. It was a terrible time for Gerry and as a young and very gifted footballer, he felt as though his world had collapsed around him. The game today has been cleaned up a lot, but you do still see the occasional bad tackle that could, as with Gerry, potentially end a player's career. In my opinion, there is just no place for it in football and it should be wiped out completely. Arguably the punishments still aren't strong enough and if a player is found guilty, he should be banned for six months without pay. With the number of cameras at football matches these days, there is a real opportunity to put a finish to career-ending tackles for good and send a message to the perpetrators – we don't want you in the game. I was pleased to know that Gerry went to America to set up business and was very successful. I was also pleased he left England as he used to beat me at golf. He had the worst slice I have ever seen and would stand square onto the ball at the tee facing in the wrong direction so he could bend the ball and it would hit the fairway. I used to find it funny when he would do this every time, but it would really wind-up some of the players he would play against. Back then, I don't think I ever beat him at golf, although with the practice I've put in over the years, I might stand a decent chance now.

The 68–69 season had started relatively well for City and I was well on my way to Alan Dicks' target of fifteen goals for the season with five goals in the first thirteen games. After beating Newport County and Middlesbrough at Ashton Gate we once again were drawn away at Leeds United, in the Third Round of the League Cup, and whilst it was a battle, was nothing compared to the season before in terms of entertainment, drama or incident. I managed to get on the score-sheet, beating Sprake at his near post, which brought a smile to my face, but it was too little too late as we went out of the cup two-one. In the past, I had been very fortunate with injuries, but unfortunately this season would be my worst from that perspective. I had already missed over a month of the season with a thigh injury, when I picked up an ankle knock away at Preston. Initially, I was unable to walk properly, but Les thought it would heal with rest and that I would be back in light training within a week and back playing in a fortnight. The gash, however, didn't heal without a hospital visit and it was eventually stitched up and put in plaster to help the process along. The plaster was removed and stitches were taken out on Christmas Eve, but by the time I was back in training, I had missed twelve matches. Almost inevitably, my return in January was the catalyst for the rumour mill and media merry-go-round to get into top gear. I scored twice and set-up three more in a six-nil hammering of Fulham at Ashton Gate. This only added to the speculation, this time Nottingham Forest sending out the scouts to watch me in action. It was all very flattering, but as a Bristol boy, all I wanted was to play for Bristol City and help them win promotion. I was happy and settled both on and off the pitch and I had recently got engaged to Trish. As the so-say 'Golden Boy' of West Country football, the papers needed no encouragement in writing another speculative article, stating that Trish and I planned to get married in the new year, shortly after my twenty-first birthday.

As well as being linked to a host of First Division clubs, I was also being talked about as a possible England Under-23 choice. The selectors had watched me shortly after my return in February when I had scored two goals in a 3–0 home win against Carlisle and would watch me several times during the season, all seemingly to no avail. Little did I know at the time that my performances for City during the 1968–69 season and my goals, along with top-scorer John Galley, that kept us in Division Two, would pay off for me on a personal level only months later. It was a very special moment in my career when I was chosen by Sir Alf Ramsey to be a member of the England Under-23 squad in a fixture against Wales. In addition to this great honour, at the relatively tender age of twenty, the game was to be played at Ashton Gate. Although I was only a substitute on this occasion, I couldn't quite believe that I was training with a squad full of such talented players and household names: Peter Shilton, Peter Osgood, Colin Todd, Tony Currie, David Nish, John Aston and Brian Kidd to name but a few. It was a proud moment just to step out of the Grand Hotel in Bristol and walk to the cinema in the centre of town with my England blazer on. Pulling on an England shirt at my home ground and looking down before the game to see the Three Lions on my chest was a fantastic feeling. Despite not actually getting on the pitch, just being involved in the build-up and the fixture itself was enough for me at that time. I was the only player from a lower division club in the squad and it gave me a taste of what it was like at the top of the game. I felt then that playing at a better standard would also benefit my own game and that the only way to get on was to play at the highest level possible. Later that season, I earned my first Under-23 cap against Bulgaria at Home Park, home of Plymouth Argyle. I came on as a second-half substitute in front of a 36,000 crowd. Although I had worn the England shirt before, the sense of immense pride on this occasion was ten-fold and was also mixed with a nervous anxiety, as I was told before the game that I would make an appearance at some point during the ninety minutes. I can't remember who I came on for, or what minute it was – to me that was completely irrelevant. As I stood on the touchline, with the linesman checking every last detail, all I wanted to do was get on the pitch, soak up the atmosphere, enjoy it and remember it forever. Somewhat predictably, the rest is a blur.

As speculated in the local press, 1970 was also a memorable year off the pitch as I married my now long-term girlfriend and fiancée of just over one year, Trish. Little did I know when we started to know each other in the Robins Café by Ashton Gate that some five or six years later we would be walking down the aisle. On 6 June 1970, I married Patricia Cooper at St Paul's Church on Coronation Road in Southville, Bristol, on a beautifully hot and sunny day. It seemed absolutely packed inside and outside the church as there was a lot of interest locally. Martin, who married Barbara during the same year, was my best man and we had four bridesmaids. In addition, many players past and present were in attendance, including my good friends Geoff Merrick and Bobby Kellard. We also invited Mr Vokes and Mr Templar, my headmaster and sports master respectively at South Street Primary School, as they had been my mentors for such a large part of my early playing career and two men to whom I owed so much. The reception was held in the lovely surroundings of The Royal Hotel on College Green, in the centre of Bristol and with about ninety guests, the bill amounted to £186! After the meal and speeches, my parents and a few others took us to Temple Meads to see us off on our honeymoon. We booked in for one week in another lovely hotel, The Imperial Hotel at Torquay, and I am told that while Trish and I were getting used to married life, the partying continued long into the night back in Bristol. After one night, Trish couldn't wait any longer to move into our recently purchased house in Long Ashton, so we cut short the honeymoon and caught the next train back to Bristol.

Unfortunately, the harmony off the football pitch couldn't be matched on the turf, with Bristol City still struggling and as a consequence my name being linked with almost every top club in the country. I have to be honest in saying that although I would have dearly loved to get to the First Division with City, I just could not see it happening. Life was still tough for the squad at the foot of the table, fighting for survival year-in, year-out. During my time in the first team at City, I knew no other kind of season. Since my debut in the 1966–67 campaign, our best finish had been fourteenth. The 1970–71 season ended in another disappointing finish in nineteenth place, but was also tinged with sadness at the terrible injury that Gerry Sharpe had picked up half way through the season. The uncertainty in Gerry's life certainly put all of our problems into perspective. John Galley, once again, topped the scoring charts with twelve goals and I wasn't far behind with eleven in all competitions. Although bitterly frustrating for players and supporters, it nevertheless meant survival for another year in the Second Division. Not long after our final league fixture, I, along with the rest of the City squad, went to Spain for an end-of-season tournament. It was a relatively uneventful tour on and off the pitch, with the exception of Gordon and a few of the boys looking for a little lad touring with the Middlesbrough party! Shortly before the end of the tour, Alan Dicks pulled me to one side to tell me he had received a telephone call from the secretary of the FA, asking me to fly back to England as soon as possible, as I had been selected to be a part of the Football Association tour of Australia. It was leaving in three days and so I had to get back as quickly as I could. Everything happened so fast that I even had to give the FA my chest, collar, waist and leg measurements over the telephone, so they could have my suit made while I was travelling back. To suddenly be called upon to go away again so soon after the Spanish tour was a bit rough on Trish as we had been married less than twelve months, but thankfully I think she knew and accepted early on that travel and staying away was all part of the life of a professional footballer.

I met up with the squad at Dublin Airport, as the fifteen other players had their first game of the tour against a Republic of Ireland XI at Lansdowne Road before making the 12,000-mile trip to Sydney. Because of the rush of returning from City's tour and the preparation needed for Australia, I was excused this game. On arrival at the airport, the secretary of the FA gave me my blazer and trousers to change into in one of the airport toilets. I couldn't believe it. It looked like a clown suit. The jacket completely covered my hands, so I had to put elastic bands around the cuffs to keep them back. It was a joke and I had to wear this for the next six weeks on tour in Australia! The blazer was only part of the story as whenever I had to wear the full outfit for official business, like meeting an Australian dignitary, the lads certainly had a good laugh at my baggy flannels as well. The tour itself went extremely well and was a fantastic experience. The manager for the tour was Ron Suart of Chelsea and his assistant was Manchester United's Wilf McGuiness. We went through the tour unbeaten, playing eight games, three of which were internationals against our hosts' full national line-up in Perth, Melbourne and Sydney. Without exception, we had fantastic ex-pat crowds wherever we played and the atmosphere was fantastic. As a late replacement, I didn't expect to be named in the starting line-up, but the manager asked if I could play on the left-hand-side of a 4-3-3 formation. Of course I said that I could and after a decent performance in the first game, I stayed in the team for the rest of the tour. We had a few jokers in the squad and the fun and laughter off the pitch certainly matched the enjoyment on the pitch. We played one game against Western Australia in Perth and there was a decent crowd of about 10,000. I went to take a corner and as I placed the ball down felt a tap on my shoulder. I looked round and saw Barry Bridges and Ken Wagstaff. 'Fancy a beer?' they asked. I couldn't believe it, they were leaning against the boards with their full kit on having a beer while they were supposed to be warming up. Ron and Wilf were so caught up in the game that they didn't realise that when they sent the subs to get warmed up, what they were really doing was getting quietly hammered in the corner of the ground out of view! It was ridiculous, particularly in an international game. I mean, could you imagine that today? I also scored what was probably the best goal of my career in one of the international matches in Melbourne. I was just inside the penalty area and made a run towards the near post. The ball was passed into my feet by Barry Bridges and I let it run through my legs and I back-heeled it into the top right-hand corner. All the lads said it was a fluke and the coaches and staff fell off the bench, but I know in my own mind that it was intentional. I turned around to celebrate by simply walking away with one arm in the air as if it was something that I did every day of the week. In many ways it was similar to the now-famous goal scored by Gianfranco Zola for Chelsea a few years ago – but better! The only possible downside was that the matches didn't count as caps back in 1971 which was a bit of a blow, but I made sure I kept all my shirts from the tour, plus an Australian blazer that I swapped for my own after the last game – a good deal in my eyes because, as well as being a memento, the Australian blazer fitted me better. Today, however, I only have one of my international shirts left. I have given a couple to charity, another to my good friend Viv Richards, and a few to family members over the years. The tour was the most wonderful experience and I really felt at home over there, particularly in beautiful Perth, where I could quite easily have settled.

I had found out whilst on tour in Spain that Leicester City had put in a bid for me. Alan Dicks pulled me to one side to tell me and virtually said that as long as the offer was between £50,000 and £100,000, City might have to accept the bid as the club needed the money. Alan told me this about the same time as I was told about my FA tour call-up and I couldn't really take it all in. However, I was well aware that, with Bristol City now looking at the possibility of letting me go, the trip to Australia was the golden opportunity to show exactly what I could do on the pitch at the highest level. In Ron Suart and Wilf McGuiness, I also had two coaches watching my every move from two of the biggest clubs in the country. On returning from a very successful tour down-under, I went straight to see Alan Dicks, who confirmed that City had received a bid of £80,000 from Leicester City. Although a good offer, the club decided to turn it down, as three or four clubs were seriously interested, and to hold out for a bid in the region of £100,000. I was then told categorically that if Bristol City received a bid of £100,000, regardless of who it was from, they would sell me. I appeared to have absolutely no say in the matter. Leicester City were favourites for a long time, despite Manchester United, through Wilf McGuiness reporting back on my progress in Australia, expressing an interest. In all the hype and speculation, City chairman Harry Dolman, a fantastic chairman and very good friend of mine, was constantly reported as saying in the press that 'Chris will not be leaving Bristol City in the near future'. I had signed a three-year contract shortly after my twenty-first birthday and there was also an option of another three years on top of that, which effectively tied me to the club for six years. Even towards the end, when it was almost inevitable that I would be leaving the club, he refused to accept the fact. Later, Marina, Harry's wife, would tell my mother that it broke his heart the day City sold me. With everything that had happened, I eventually asked to be placed on the transfer list in an attempt to end the uncertainty, but despite this, nothing was agreed before the start of the 1971–72 season and I prepared as normal for the forthcoming campaign. Unlike recent seasons, we started well and I scored three goals in the first four games against Middlesbrough, Cardiff City and Sheffield Wednesday. We were unbeaten and there was further speculation about my staying in Bristol. In addition to the firm bid from Leicester City, City also had received an offer of £100,000 from Chelsea. With Ron Suart's connections at Chelsea and my experience on the FA tour, I thought that going to west London would be an excellent move for me. On the morning of Wednesday, 1 September 1971, Alan Dicks called me into his office and told me that Bristol City had officially accepted Chelsea's £100,000 bid and asked if I would be interested in signing for them. Although I was reluctant to leave the club I had supported and dreamt of playing for since a child, I had also dreamt of playing at the highest level in England since my school days. It was another dream come true and I accepted Alan's proposal. The contract I had recently signed at City was worth £50 per week, raised from £25. The deal I was offered at Chelsea was £80 per week and I also received five per cent of the transfer fee spread over my two-year contract. As with the tour of Australia, Trish was supportive of my move to London. She knew that as a twenty-two year-old footballer, I wanted to play at the highest level possible, and if that meant moving then it was something we had to do. The same afternoon, I got into Alan's Rover and pulled away from Ashton Gate one last time. It was an incredibly strange feeling. He drove us to Stamford Bridge to complete the deal.

On arrival at Stamford Bridge, I was taken through to meet Dave Sexton, at which point I realised that I was on my own. Alan Dicks suddenly went missing and I certainly didn't have an agent. I have made mistakes with contracts throughout my career and in the heat and excitement of the situation, I made one almighty 'balls-up' yet again at Chelsea – I signed a blank contract. Everything had happened so quickly that nothing had been officially prepared and the personal terms offered to me initially were purely verbal. At the time I didn't really care, I just signed the contract and said that I wanted to play for Chelsea and they could fill it in later. Dave Sexton couldn't believe it. 'Christ, that's the first time anyone has ever said that to me. You're gonna have to learn fast here son, with the likes of Peter Osgood and Ron Harris about', he replied.

As a £100,000 signing, it was a lot of money and a lot of pressure, but I was looking forward to the challenge as I travelled back up to London the following day to be introduced to the squad and staff. I was put up in a lovely hotel in the West End for a couple of nights, before being swiftly brought back down to earth on the third day. I was taken over to Mitcham and put up in a standard terraced bed and breakfast where I would stay for about two months with a South African lad called Derek Smethurst who was a Chelsea reserve team player. He didn't talk to me when I moved in as I was a forward and so was he, and he thought I had come to take his place in the pecking order. To top that, the two ladies running the B&B were lesbians and school dinner ladies who used to bring the left-over school dinners home, warm them up and give them to us as our evening meal! I figured out what was going on straightaway and I took a carrier bag with me to dinner. I used to shove it all in the bag, say thank-you and then head straight for the Aberdeen Angus Steak House about half-a-mile away. I was beginning to realise what Dave Sexton meant about learning quickly off the field and, in a completely different environment from what I had come to expect in Bristol, the lessons were coming thick and fast. I was away from my family and friends in a city I knew little about, but consoled myself with the thought that I was a First Division player and, as 'the kid from the sticks', I would soon be competing and playing with the very best players that England had to offer.

CHAPTER THREE

TAXI TO THE BRIDGE

Everything had happened so swiftly that I was in a daze and almost punch-drunk from all the excitement and goings on of the first few days in London. After travelling up with Alan on the Wednesday, I had signed within twenty minutes. I stayed on to watch Chelsea's fixture with West Bromwich Albion that evening before heading back to Bristol to say my goodbyes. Everything had changed so suddenly that when I was back in Bristol that night, I really had to question whether any of it had actually happened. With the large squad of very talented players at Stamford Bridge, I assumed that I would have a couple of weeks to settle in and find my feet before fighting for my place in the team. I travelled back up to west London the next day and started training straight away. I felt the first training session went well and was introduced to all the players. I didn't know what to expect from the other squad members upon my arrival and was nervous about any backlash from the major personalities in the camp. After winning the FA Cup in 1970 and the European Cup Winners' Cup in 1971 and finishing a respectable sixth in the league, I'm sure that many of the squad wondered what use a country bumpkin from the West Country would be to a club like Chelsea. After the successes of the previous years, many of the squad questioned why Dave Sexton felt the need to go out and buy players at all. If I am completely honest, it took a long time for the players to accept me.

Within a week or so, Sexton had also signed Steve Kember from Crystal Palace, which was a huge positive for me as I had known Steve since our England Youth team days and still kept in touch. Despite signing from another London club, I think even Steve found it difficult initially, but we often helped each other out. To say the other players gave us the cold shoulder would be a little bit harsh, but if you wanted to be a part of the club, you really had to earn their respect. Little groups of players would appear around the club and

40

you often wondered if there was something that you were missing out on. Peter Osgood was one of the superstars of the side and he had his hangers-on and likewise with Alan Hudson and Dave Webb. I, on the other hand, had no hangers-on because I just didn't know anybody. The established players had almost an impenetrable group around them and if they played well they would get a pat on the back from their 'friends' and head towards the King's Road. If they played badly, they would still get a pat on the back from their 'friends' and head towards the King's Road!

Chelsea and Chelsea Football Club have always symbolised wealth, fashion, style and the high-life. This arguably reached its pinnacle in 2005 with Roman Abramovich's investment ultimately bringing success. Back in 1971, despite football as a business being very different, the King's Road was still the epicentre of 'cool' and the place to be seen. Whether you went with friends or team mates, you were eating in the very best restaurants, wearing expensive clothes and paying £12 for a haircut! I pay about half that amount now for a haircut all these years on, and back then it was a case of 'don't take too much off' as long hair was the fashion. They would literally give you a trim and blow dry and charge you for the privilege of being in a barber's shop on the King's Road. All of this highlights (and I had plenty of them as well!) how money was spent and the lifestyles, even in those days, we all led as professional footballers. Dave Sexton had said I had to learn quickly. Peter Osgood mentioned that when I arrived at Stamford Bridge I looked more like I'd stepped off Bondi Beach than a top footballer. I did have a loud jacket and always felt that I had dressed well (something my parents had instilled in me from an early age), but after that it was flares, frills, collars and kipper ties all the way!

The adjustment off the pitch was always going to take time, but on the pitch was a completely different matter. My expectation of a 'settling in period' was thrown up in the air on my second day of training. We trained at Stamford Bridge on the Friday and when the team was posted for the following day's fixture at home to Coventry City, I couldn't believe my eyes – I was included in the starting line-up. Alan Hudson had been sent home with a temperature, so I had been thrust straight into the action. I would partner Peter Osgood, who, after previously falling out with manager Dave Sexton, had, after pressure from supporters, been taken off the transfer list during the week I had signed for Chelsea. After a shaky start to the season, when Chelsea had lost 0–3 and 2–3 to Arsenal and Manchester United respectively, the team had picked up recently, winning their last two fixtures against Huddersfield and West Brom. On the Saturday morning, I made my own way to the ground, taking a short taxi journey from the hotel I was staying in and we had a meal in another hotel just off the Fulham Road. As you would expect, I was excited at the thought of making my debut and, as with many of the big games in my career to date, the 'nerves' I should have experienced were replaced with eager anticipation. I just wanted to get on with the match.

I was more than pleased with this first game for Chelsea and had to wait only four minutes to make my first major contribution, laying on the ball for Peter Osgood to score. Some hacks in the media had previously dubbed Ossie 'The King of Stamford Bridge', and the following day they declared me 'The Crown Prince'. I wondered if maybe it wouldn't take as long to be accepted by the fans and the media! ITV also covered the highlights of the match that evening and commentator Brian Moore said that Stamford Bridge had a new hero. I thought this was maybe premature, but it was still nice to hear after only a few days with my new employers. The remainder of my debut was one hell of a game and it was fantastic to experience top-flight football. The match finished 3–3 and I had experienced the chasm between the First and Second Divisions in England. The class of player you are playing with and against every week, the speed of the game and the consistently high standard of football week-in week-out were far superior to anything I had experienced. After the Coventry game, Dave Sexton seemed pleased with my performance and everyone seemed happy with my contribution, but I didn't play again for the first team for several games. I knew that when Chelsea bought me I would be a squad player, competing with the likes of Ian Hutchinson and Tommy Baldwin for a place in the starting line-up, but it was still disappointing after such a promising first outing. When I did get my next opportunity, it was against Nottingham Forest in the Third Round of the League Cup. Unfortunately, my return lasted only half-an-hour. I received the ball just inside the Forest half, but as I turned, I was hit late with a bad tackle by Barry Lyons. As I lay on the turf, I could see that the tackle had caused a clash between the two sets of players. I limped off the pitch to play no further part, only to be joined some ten minutes later by Lyons – on a stretcher. Ron 'Chopper' Harris had taken Lyons' number after his tackle on me, and then promptly lived up to his nickname. The match ended 1–1 and whilst Barry Lyons was fit to play in the replay, I had my ankle put in plaster for a few days to immobilise the joint and didn't play again for over a month. I took the opportunity to return home to Bristol for a few days, to see Trish and my parents, and rest the injury properly.

While I was fighting for fitness and a place in the team, my private life was at its busiest. After I'd spent around six weeks in digs, Trish and I eventually found the house we liked in Chessington. It was important to get settled because Trish was due to give birth to our first child at any moment. We sold our house in Long Ashton, Bristol for £4,200 making about £2,000 profit, and purchased a three-bedroom black wood, Victorian-style semi-detached house in Chessington for £10,550. It doesn't sound a lot now, but it was a five-times hike on our mortgage payments. My wages certainly hadn't increased at the same rate as I had been on £50 a week at City and now £80 at Chelsea. However, the major financial difference between the two clubs was the bonus structure. At Bristol City I used to get £4 for a win and £2 for a draw. At Chelsea we were on £80-a-point, meaning I could double my basic salary with a draw! Having sold the house for some £18,500 when I eventually left Chelsea, I was absolutely devastated to hear that in the last few years, the owners had sold it for nearly £500,000! The house was to the south-west of Chelsea and was close enough to the ground, but far enough away to be able to escape the pace of the city. In addition, it was just a short drive from Sandown Park racecourse in Esher.

Trish travelled back to Bristol towards the end of October to give birth at Bristol Maternity Hospital and be near family and friends. When I first signed for Chelsea, it was a difficult time initially, not only for me in a new environment, but for Trish who was over one hundred miles away in Bristol. The reason for all the worrying and the travelling certainly became clear when Adam Christopher was born at Bristol Maternity Hospital on 31 October weighing a healthy 9lb 2oz. It was a wonderful feeling and I couldn't wait for the moment when I could finally take Trish and Adam back home to Chessington.

On regaining my fitness, I had been a member of the Chelsea first-team squad during my time out of the side and continued to work hard in training. However, by the middle of December 1971 I had been

offered few opportunities to shine, playing in just two League games
and two League Cup matches. It was now three months since my last
outing, but Dave Sexton eventually gave me the nod to make my next
appearance and I was keen to impress and take my chance. I really
couldn't have asked for a bigger game to make my reappearance, as
we were playing Tottenham Hotspur in the semi-final first leg of the
League Cup. I was fortunate that I had not been cup-tied with Bristol
City, as I had missed their First Round match through injury. With
Steve Kember cup-tied and Tommy Baldwin still struggling with a leg
injury that had plagued his season, not only did I have a chance to earn
a place in the side on a regular basis, I also had a major opportunity
to stake my claim for a possible Wembley place should we overcome
Spurs. A crowd of 43,000 turned up at Stamford Bridge on
Wednesday, 22 December 1971 to watch us beat Spurs 3–2 and give
us a slender advantage going into the second leg. From a personal
perspective it was a success also. With Tottenham 2–1 up, I scored the
equaliser after seventy-five minutes with a header, which put us right
back into an often ill-tempered match that we looked to be losing.
John Hollins then scored from the penalty spot with five minutes to
go, giving us what had seemed an unlikely victory. The second leg at
White Hart Lane two weeks later drew an attendance of nearly 53,000
and, as with the first leg, was an ill-tempered game. Again, we went
behind, this time to a Martin Chivers goal on the stroke of half-time.
After the break, we came out a different side and created numerous
chances before I scored the equaliser after sixty-three minutes. In my
eyes, it was one of the best goals of my career. Firstly because it was
a cup semi-final, but also because it was a left-footed shot from
twenty-five yards which scorched past the great Pat Jennings, who
was left stranded. Spurs went ahead again on the night with only eight
minutes remaining through a Martin Peters strike from the penalty
spot, levelling the tie 4–4 on aggregate. The home crowd were still
celebrating when, with only two minutes on the clock, Alan Hudson
hit a low free-kick towards the Tottenham goal, Cyril Knowles missed
his kick and the ball went in off the post, sending the tremendous
travelling Chelsea following wild. The last few minutes seemed to
take hours, but finally referee Mr Smith blew the full-time whistle and
we had made it to the final of the League Cup. Whilst I was overjoyed
at reaching a Wembley final, there was also a huge sense of relief on
my part that I had been given an opportunity in two big games and

taken my chance, scoring in both legs. Until then, the headlines and articles in the local and national press were starting to question my ability and whether I had what it took to play in the First Division. Some said I had a 'walk-on part' at Chelsea whilst others referred to me as 'the £100,000 substitute', neither of which I could argue with at the time, but all I needed was a chance and thankfully the semi-final matches provided the opening. As a consequence, I thought that maybe I had proved my point that I deserved my place in the team. As I sat in the dressing room after the game, it suddenly dawned on me, 'Christ, we're at Wembley'. I had achieved my first ambition of playing for Bristol City, my second of pulling on an England shirt and wearing the Three Lions and now I had reached my next goal of playing in a Wembley final – all by the age of twenty-two. Although it was a dream of mine to play at Wembley, I never really thought it would happen. It just didn't seem to happen to lads brought up in Bedminster and Ashton. The only downside was that I had taken a knock to my ankle towards the end of the game and hobbled out of White Hart Lane with my foot in a slipper. With competition for places so fierce at Stamford Bridge, the last thing I needed was an injury, particularly at a time when I had fought for my place in the side, but the blow to the ankle would keep me out for three matches. Nevertheless, after the game we headed back to the King's Road from north London and a few of us descended on our favourite restaurant, Alexander's, to celebrate reaching the final. Alexander's was owned and run by several gay men, rare in the early 1970s as society wasn't as accepting of homosexuals as it is today. The restaurant was superb and the food always excellent and a haunt we would revisit time and again. We had a few drinks and a meal and by 2.30am it was time to go. It may seem rather late, particular for a 'school night', but in reality we had been at the restaurant for around three hours. By the time we had showered and changed, given interviews and made our way back across London, it was already getting late. One or two of us had taken our cars to Alexander's and before we got in the cabs booked to take us home, we went to check that they were locked up. Peter Osgood had a signed match ball from the night's game in his car and went to get it as he didn't want to leave it in there overnight. Signed match balls often prove to be quite valuable, particularly from a semi-final and can raise a lot of money for charity. Unfortunately for Ossie, the police turned up. As we had walked to the cars, we were singing Chelsea songs in celebration and apparently the police had received complaints. We told them that we were in high spirits after reaching the final, but not causing any trouble. One of the many coppers that attended said to Ossie, 'Just get in your car and go home'. At that moment, one of Ossie's mates stepped in, realising that if he'd have put one foot in his car they'd have nicked him for drink-driving. A bit of a ruck started and, as it was his mate in the middle of it all, Ossie went over and tried to calm things down, only to get arrested. A few of us went with him to the police station and they charged Ossie with being drunk and disorderly. I eventually got home at about 5am, but had to report to the Court the next day as a witness. The police asked me how much Ossie had to drink and I could honestly say that I only saw him have a couple of halves of lager and a glass of champagne. I could say that honestly because he had sat on a different table to me. Knowing Ossie, it was probably more likely to have been two bottles of champagne or two gallons of beer, but I could only say what I saw. The case was eventually thrown out of court and rightly so, but that didn't stop the tabloids making a big story out of it. While my estimate of the quantities may have been slightly out – well, we were drunk after all – the fact of the matter was that we weren't upsetting anybody and Peter was never going to drive that night. Some might suggest it was an attempt by the officers on duty, who possibly supported another London club, to stitch up a big-name footballer. I couldn't possibly comment!

My next target after the semi-final was to be in the starting line-up at Wembley on 4 March. It gave me the opportunity to get a few games under my belt and fight for my place in the two months leading up to the final. I was still very fit, as I had worked hard with Dave Sexton in training and also in reserve team fixtures, but I rarely enjoyed playing for the second string. There was no crowd, no atmosphere and it was a bit disheartening at times, but I knew I had to wait for my chance and thankfully it had come at the right time.

I talked earlier about the image and style of Chelsea and even in the four months I had been with the club I had noticed the 'show business' air around the ground. Many stars came to Stamford Bridge to watch games, including actress Raquel Welch and actor Michael Crawford. Director Richard Attenborough was a major celebrity in his own right. Some of the players enjoyed living up to the 'show-biz' tag attached to the football club and they enjoyed the lifestyle that came with it. Leading up to the Cup Final, an opportunity came to light that would really catapult the team into the pop star life. I'm not sure exactly who decided, but some of the players were asked about making a Cup Final record. Before we knew it, a date had been set of Thursday 4 February to record the song 'Blue is the Colour'. We were also booked to be on 'Top of the Pops'. We had to be at the BBC studios at Television Centre at 10am for rehearsals, as the show would go out live later that evening. All the players turned up, along with hangers-on, and the drinking started almost as soon as we got there. While we were rehearsing the song, I have never seen so many crates of lager drunk in one day in my life. The rest of the line-up on the show, including the dancers Pan's People and Gilbert O'Sullivan, must have wondered who this rowdy bunch of drunks were. In an attempt at least to look the part, someone had gone to a clothes shop nearby and returned with identical polo-neck jumpers for us all to wear. By the time it came to actually performing on the show, the alcohol had started to take control and if players weren't running amuck in the studios, they were slumped in a corner, unable to stand, let alone sing. Four or five of the lads were just too hammered to take their place in front of the television cameras. We made up the numbers with a few of the friends who'd come with us. Chelsea fans watching the show must have wondered what the hell was going on and where the other players were. Nevertheless, the song was released on 21 February and reached a high of number five in the charts, enjoying a twelve-week stay in the top forty.

Around this time, I made one of my frequent return visits to Bristol to catch up with family and friends. On this occasion, I also attended a Sporting Dinner at Redwood Lodge Hotel and Country Club on the outskirts of Bristol. Brian Clough was the guest speaker and during a question-and-answer session at the end of the evening, I took the opportunity to ask his opinion on a footballing issue. 'Mr Clough,' I started, in a desperate attempt to show my respect. 'Don't you think transfer fees are too high these days? For example I have just been transferred to Chelsea for £100,000.' Clough replied without a moment's thought, 'Well, that's way too much for you lad, sit down and have another drink.' Slightly embarrassed, I took my seat. Thankfully I got the chance to get my own back a few months later, when we played Clough's Derby County. I scored twice in the match and after the game he came into our dressing room and gave me a knowing wink.

Training on a Friday was at Stamford Bridge and Dave Sexton came up with an idea to make it even more competitive than it already was. The day before a match it was lighter training, generally sprints and five-a-side. The five-a-sides were on the concrete of the car park, with the turnstiles often getting in the way. Around two hundred people would come to watch these games as they weren't your ordinary five-a-sides. Dave's idea was to create two sets of players; the Goodies and the Baddies and he produced t-shirts with the names on the front. This wound people up even more and the fact it was played on concrete had little relevance. I was on the Goodies team along with guys like Steve Kember, John Hollins, Paddy Mulligan and Dave Webb. The Baddies included Ossie and Ron Harris among others. The games were horrendous and, bearing in mind this was the day before a game, some of the tackles and challenges resulted in more broken noses and knocks than you would get on a Saturday.

One week before the League Cup Final we had another important cup match, this time away to Second Division Orient in the Fifth Round of the FA Cup. On paper, it was a game that should have been comfortable for a Chelsea team made up of so many household names, but unfortunately that was also the attitude of a number of players in the squad going into the match. I was named as substitute and while I wasn't particularly happy, I looked upon the positive aspect that at least I would avoid injury and stand a chance of being called up for the final. After going two-nil up against Orient through Dave Webb and Ossie, we were cruising going into half-time and the match that appeared comfortable on paper looked to be transferring itself on the pitch. Just before the break, however, Orient pulled one back, putting a different complexion on the second half. To make matters worse, Orient equalised three minutes into the second period. With the game heading to a replay at Stamford Bridge, unusually sloppy defending once again cost us dearly and Orient striker Barrie Fairbrother popped up to score the winner with only a minute remaining. The dressing room after the match wasn't a place for the faint-hearted. Everyone was disgusted with the performance and the fact that we had let a two-goal lead slip away against a team one division below us. After the anger and disappointment of being knocked out of the FA Cup, it still remained that on the following Saturday, we were in the League Cup Final and we quickly had to rediscover the belief and mentality to win.

Although I had played, and played well, in a few League Cup games in the run up to Wembley, plus the fact that the team had suffered a setback the week before, I didn't honestly think I would be included in the starting eleven for the final and was resigned to hoping for a place on the bench. Prior to the Orient game, there was almost an uncomfortable feeling at the club, one of over-confidence from some corners of the dressing room. We were playing Stoke City in the final and the feeling was that Stoke had nothing that could possibly bother Chelsea. They had one or two good players and the best goalkeeper in the world, but we're Chelsea! In my experience, over-confidence can often be worse than having no confidence at all and the result against Orient certainly brought a few members of the squad back down to earth with a bump. On the Monday morning, Dave Sexton called a players' meeting to try and clear the air. In addition, Dave did something which was highly unusual for him on the Wednesday – he named the team for the final. Since I had been at the club, the team was always announced on the Saturday. Moreover, my name was on the sheet of paper. 'Great, I'm involved,' I thought, after scouring the sheet for anything that even slightly resembled 'Garland'. Having looked a little closer, I realised that not only was I involved, but I was actually starting the match. I had to keep looking at the team sheet to make sure I hadn't misread it. My mind went back again to growing up in south Bristol and all the people I had told as a young boy that I was going to be a professional footballer. I know that a lot of youngsters say that and I was just one of the lucky ones out of the thousands good enough, but I wasn't a very confident lad and never really thought it would happen to me. In my own mind, it almost seemed like a fairytale and now, in front of 100,000 fans and millions on television, I would be running out at Wembley.

We were given six complimentary tickets and about one hundred tickets each were put aside for us to buy. Stan Flashman was a well known businessman and ticket tout, particularly in the Capital and for some players getting to a Cup Final was a big pay day. Stan would go to see Chelsea's own 'ticket distributor' known as 'The Fox', and some players could make a lot of money selling their tickets – up to £4,000 for a Cup Final. When 'The Fox' wasn't playing for Chelsea, he could often be found on the Fulham Road selling tickets before a game. I wasn't that way inclined and I knew in my own mind where the majority of them were going and had already given away eighty of the one hundred tickets to family and friends before I knew I was playing. In addition, we had arranged the christening of our first child, Adam, on the Sunday after the Cup Final, which also coincided with Trish's twenty-first birthday a few days earlier on the 2 March. The christening was the perfect opportunity for all our family and friends to get together. They could watch the game on the Saturday and then stay over for the christening.

Concerned about my lack of games in the first team – due to niggling injuries and the team performing well – Dave Sexton arranged a special practice session for me a few days before the final. I trained for the best part of two hours with Eddie McCreadie, Dave Webb, Dave Sexton and his assistant Ron Suart, during which time I was the central figure in every move we rehearsed. The rest of the squad had the day off and I was glad of the individual workout. I walked off the training pitch knowing in my own mind that I was 100% ready for the final. I slept surprisingly well the night before the final but, rather like a child on Christmas Day, I couldn't wait for morning to come and the excitement to begin. Our journey from the hotel to Wembley was relatively uneventful, but a now familiar air of confidence was bubbling inside the team coach. When we arrived, we embarked on the walk around the ground, looking at the sheer size of the magnificent stadium towering above us and the perfect, lush green grass under our feet. The changing rooms were also superb and after our stroll, we began to get focussed on the job in hand. Walking down the long tunnel into the sunlight and the roar of the crowd was a fantastic experience and one I will never forget. I had an idea where my parents were sitting and as we proudly walked across the turf, I looked up into the stands hoping to see them. Sure enough, I found them in an instant and beamed towards them with a broad smile on my face. It was a wonderful day and the only thing that let us down was the result – we lost 2–1. My memories of the day and the match itself are extremely vague. I can remember walking out and later walking up the steps to collect my runners-up tankard, but it is almost as if the game didn't happen. When I look back at the recording of the game now, I am pleased with my own performance, as I dimly was at the time, and was unofficially named man-of-the-match. Gordon Banks had a tremendous game in the Stoke City goal. He pulled off a string of fine saves, including one diving at my feet in injury time, proving that he was the world's best keeper. It was nice to know that I didn't freeze under the circumstances, but unfortunately one or two of our lads did, and several players went out on the Friday night, treating it like any other, by having a few drinks and staying out later than they should. On this occasion, they let the rest of us down. It doesn't matter if you are playing Liverpool, Manchester United or even Bristol Rovers, you don't go out and abuse yourself the night before a game. At the final whistle, I was gutted that we had lost, but also felt that, from a selfish perspective, I had done myself justice and not let anyone down. I still think it was one of the best performances of my career.

Ironically, the Chelsea directors had booked the Hilton Hotel on Park Lane for a lavish victory celebration party. The possibility of losing the match simply never crossed their minds. Despite the result, the manager wanted all the players at the hotel for the 'party'. Initially the mood was sombre, as you would imagine, but as the alcohol began to flow and, Chelsea being Chelsea, so the atmosphere changed. I, of course, was hoping for a treble celebration that weekend, with a win in the Cup Final, Trish's twenty-first birthday and the christening of Adam. This wasn't to be, but I still had a full day ahead the next day and so left the Hilton with the revelry still in full swing.

I was determined to enjoy the following day regardless of the result, as there were many members of the family and friends making the journey from Bristol to Chessington for the christening. Both Trish and I were delighted that our close friends Bobby Kellard and Steve Carey had agreed to be Adam's godfathers. It was a long but lovely day and it meant that I certainly didn't have time to sit and dwell on the happenings of the day before.

The remainder of the season was all about finishing off our league campaign in the best manner we could. We had already been knocked out of two other cup competitions by teams that Chelsea Football Club should have beaten – losing in the Fifth Round of the FA Cup to Second Division Orient and in the Second Round of the European Cup Winners Cup to a little-known Swedish side called Atvidaberg. Reaching the final of the League Cup hardly made up for all the disappointments, but we owed it to the fans and ourselves to finish as high up the league as possible and push for a UEFA Cup place. We eventually finished seventh, one place below and three points fewer than the 1970–71 season. I had managed to establish myself as a regular in the side and felt things were progressing well and I was improving all the time. Manager Dave Sexton also announced that we would be going on an end-of-season tour to Barbados. My eyes lit up as I'd never been to the Caribbean before. My experiences of end-of-season-tours or pre-season tours were more likely to have been to Torremolinos, Weston-super-Mare or Severn Beach!

We flew out to Barbados a few days after our final game of the season away at Leeds United. When we arrived in the Caribbean, we stayed in a wonderful hotel right on the beach and had two weeks to switch off and relax. We did play two matches against the island team while we were there, but when it came to these games, it was a wonder that we could get eleven players on the pitch. The first couple of days really set the tone and the standard for the two weeks. When the lads said they were going to switch off, they really meant it. It was almost like a two-week stag party and Eddie McCreadie, Charlie Cooke, Ossie and Tommy Baldwin among others, were at the forefront of everything. I'd never seen anything quite like it. After three or four days we were due to play our first match, but I think Eddie must have been sellotaped to the pool bar. Rarely did you see him away from the bar and he must have drunk enough in the first few days to sink a small island. Charlie and Tommy would disappear for a time and then return slightly worse for a cocktail or ten. I tended to spend most of my time with Steve Kember and Micky Droy, 'The Gentle Giant.' In the drinking stakes, I was way behind the others. I enjoyed a few drinks but if I was a racehorse, I would be a novice hurdler compared to these seasoned chasers. Having been at the club for only eight months, I was still unsure as to exactly what was acceptable and what crossed the line. As it turned out, I needn't have worried. So long as the group didn't upset any other guests at the resort, the management tended to turn a blind eye to the drinking and pretty much everything else, and you were free to spend the time as you wished. The matches themselves were a nightmare. We'd been on the booze for three days solid and despite the games being played at 6pm it was still too hot. Around three thousand supporters turned up, a good attendance considering the island had a population of around 250,000 which was about half the size of Bristol at the time. We won the game comfortably by four or five goals and the lads then returned to enjoying their holiday.

If you have ever been to Barbados, you would have heard about and maybe experienced *The Jolly Roger*. It is a pirate ship which takes

Swotting up in the library at Ashton Vale Junior School.

Bucket-and-spade time on Weymouth beach with brother Martin (right).

A day trip to London with Mum and Martin.

South Street Juniors – I'm in the back row, far right.

My first official team photograph – the South Street School football team.
(That's me, second left, front row)

The school's Intermediate side (1960/1),
I'm the youngest player in the team (front row, second from right).

Taken from another team
photo at ten-years-old.

On scouts' camp at Exmouth.

Mum and Dad.

An unusual team photograph from my early days at Bristol City.
I am alongside City legend John Atyeo (8).

On the verge of the first team.

Ball control for the photographers.

City's forward line, from the left: Alan Skirton, John Galley,
Bobby Kellard, myself and Gerry Sharpe.

Shooting for goal (white shirt).

Mate John Galley challenges the keeper.

Local derby with Cardiff City at Ashton Gate. My old home, aka Nelson
Mandela House, in the background. Photograph taken pre-Dolman Stand.

John Galley and I challenge in the air against Blackpool at Ashton Gate.

Scoring against Cardiff City at Ashton Gate.

Heading for goal at Ninian Park.

Flat out, courtesy of a whack from Gary Sprake in a cup tie at Elland Road.

With the Football Association representative side in Melbourne and I celebrate one of the best goals I've ever scored.

Ready for another season at Ashton Gate.

A family gathering, with dad, sister-in-law Barbara, myself, mum and brother Martin.

New boy at Chelsea.

Picking myself up from another foul, this time by Villa's Dennis Mortimer.

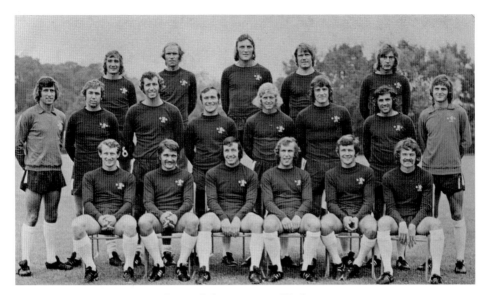

One of the team at Chelsea.

A goal for Chelsea.

Chelsea pin-up boy.

A souvenir ticket stub from our League Cup final.
Note the cost of a seat – just £1.50!

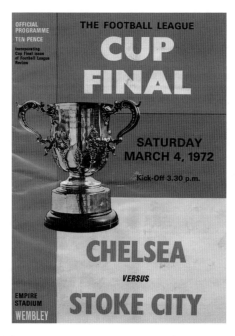

And the match-day programme from that final.

tourists off-shore with the intention of getting all on-board so drunk that you forget who you are and where you are. Four of the lads thought it would be a laugh and booked themselves on a trip. Chelsea fans of the time could probably guess the four involved. The quantities the boys drank were, by all accounts, obscene and it was the first time that *The Jolly Roger* had run clean out of vodka. They came back to the hotel full of their achievement, which was certainly no mean feat, and carried on where they left off at the hotel bar. How the lads stayed upright, I just don't know. I would have been flat on my back hours ago, but then again, I was never a real spirits drinker. One thing is for sure, if they had league tables for drinkers, these four would be getting silverware every season. Later that evening, Charlie and Tommy decided to go for a swim to see if they could climb aboard one of the many yachts that moored in the bay. How they didn't drown after drinking as they had all day, I really don't know. They swam out about fifty yards and we watched them climb aboard a boat. The rest of us went for something to eat and that was the last we saw of Tommy and Charlie until the following morning. Dave Sexton and Ron Suart liked to go for a run along the beach every morning at about seven o'clock. On this occasion, they got to the end of the beach and noticed seven or eight wild dogs asleep and curled up next to each other. At that moment Ron noticed a human leg protruding from the dogs and went over to look at closer quarters. As Ron approached, the animals woke and ran away, leaving Tommy Baldwin and Charlie Cooke on the beach fast asleep. It was a wonder that they hadn't been eaten to death. Dave and Ron couldn't believe their eyes and went ballistic. Tommy and Charlie were fined and warned about their future behaviour, which they couldn't really complain about, as the case for the defence didn't really hold much water, even though Tommy's nickname was 'The Sponge'.

A few days later, the squad were invited to the Prime Minister of Barbados' house for a formal welcoming to the island. It was all very nice, but unfortunately the tea party rapidly went downhill as a few of the lads started to hit the alcohol as usual. Lots of plants in the residence were being 'unofficially watered' which you just don't do at the home of the Prime Minister. The worst incident occurred as the Prime Minister's wife was having a conversation with the wife of the Chelsea chairman when one of the players exposed himself. Luckily enough, the chairman's wife, who was particularly good-humoured and understanding, remarked, 'Oh put that away will you. I've seen bigger things crawl out of cheese,' which fortunately took the heat out of that situation. It totally embarrassed the player involved. Needless to say, all the culprits were fined – for the second time in some cases – and for one or two players, this trip was becoming increasingly expensive. The serious drinking culture at the club was frustrating for the other members of the squad and it makes you wonder exactly how good some of the players could have been without the drink inside them.

A few of the players held grudges towards the manager and drinking to excess when it wasn't appropriate – be it on a Friday night or whilst on tour – was their way of showing their discontent. We used to train at Mitcham, not far from my initial digs, but if you were injured you attended Stamford Bridge. It took me a while to work out that several players often had knocks at the same time, were having fifteen minutes of physio on an 'injury' and then heading for the King's Road. Mitcham was miles away from Stamford Bridge and players knew they could get away with it.

After a hectic season, both on and off the pitch, we arranged a family holiday that summer to Torremolinos in Spain. It was through Pontins in the resort and many footballers were allowed to stay there free of charge. We went with Peter Osgood and Ron Harris and their families and met Denis Law and Paddy Crerand over there. It was a million miles from the team holidays. It was a relaxing break and nice to get away and spend some quality time with Trish and Adam, but in the back of my mind I was only too aware that the new season was just around the corner. I was determined to earn my place in the team and stay there. Consequently, I started pre-season training two weeks early at home, in order to give myself a slight head start. Moreover, Trish was expecting our second child, making the win bonuses even more important! Pre-season training was still tough and usually we would run cross-country in the morning and change to ball work in the afternoon. We used to go to Epsom Racecourse for our cross-country runs and I hated every minute of it – fifty-yard sprints were more my thing. Peter 'The Cat' Bonetti, on the other hand, would always win the race by a mile. After a while, Dave Sexton decided to bring in a handicap system, whereby the slower runners like Ossie and Dave Webb would go off first and 'The Cat' would start last. I thought I'd catch Ossie within a mile or so, but after a mile-and-a-half, he was still nowhere to be seen. What we didn't realise at the time was that there was a pub at the far end of Epsom Downs. The lads hid in the trees and waited for everyone to run past before strolling over to the pub for a pint of 'shandy'. After about an hour, they came running in with their shirt covered in water to make it look like they had been sweating. After the run, we headed back to the training ground at Mitcham in the van, but after about five minutes of the journey, Ron Suart, who was driving the van, caught a whiff of alcohol in the air. When we arrived in Mitcham, the players involved picked up another fine as well as a bollocking. Sexton asked them how they paid for the drinks. 'The landlord was a Chelsea supporter, so there was no problem there,' replied Ossie. Needless to say, that was the last time we had a handicap system in cross-country.

After my first season, the one thing I had to accept was that I was never going to be in the same league as some of the players at Chelsea when it came to natural ability. Their skill levels were superior and even if I trained all day, every day, there would have still been a gulf. I trained and worked hard, had two good feet and basically I made the best of what I had. Even today, if someone comes up to me in a pub or on the street and says 'you were a really good player,' it is one of the biggest compliments that anyone can pay, because I worked for it. The term 'great' is frequently over-used today. It would be wrong for me to compare different eras and the likes of Ossie and Jimmy Greaves *were* very good players. However, for me, Pele, George Best, Stanley Matthews and Tom Finney are true greats. *Webster's Dictionary* gives one definition of 'great' as being 'remarkable in ability and character' and this I feel, is the perfect description for four legends of the game in my eyes. Of the four players, 'Bestie' was the only one that I played against. He was fantastic and it often amuses me when people compare David Beckham to him today. For me there simply is no comparison. Beckham is a terrific passer of the ball and hits a great free-kick, but George could go past people, tackle, head the ball and was brave. I dreaded playing against him. He was always looking to take the piss out of me and if he didn't nutmeg me at least twice during a game he was having an off day. When I played against him for the first time at Old Trafford, Dave Sexton told me I was playing wide on the right and my heart sank, 'Oh, no, Bestie's wide on the left', I thought. The problems that George encountered off the field have been well documented, but I just want to remember him and respect him as a great friend and a terrific footballer.

A few weeks before the new season started, the club arranged a short pre-season tour of Holland, Germany and France. The tour was completely different to the trip to Barbados – we trained hard and played some tough matches against some of the finest teams in Europe. On returning to London, there was an optimistic mood about the place. In addition, chairman Brian Mears had announced previously the redevelopment of Stamford Bridge into a 60,000-capacity stadium. The work would cost around £5.5m and was planned to be completed by the end of the decade. It was a breathtaking vision and when completed, Stamford Bridge would become one of *the* premier arenas in Britain. The only downside to the plans was the disruption and inconvenience the building work caused. Stands were being pulled down, players were getting changed in portakabins and suddenly the visionary stadium seemed years away.

We couldn't really have asked for a tougher start as our first game of the 1972–73 season was at home to Leeds United and Stamford Bridge was almost unrecognisable. Nevertheless, over 51,000 fans pushed and squeezed their way into the three-sided building site to gain the best vantage point. Reports after the match suggested a further 10,000 fans were locked out. There was certainly no love lost between Chelsea and Leeds and the fact that Leeds had won the FA Cup and finished runners-up in the league the previous season made us all the more determined to get a result. I'd had my own problems over the years with various Leeds players, so I needed no incentive to be up for the game. I was selected to start the match and right from the kick-off you could sense the volatile atmosphere between the two sets of players. Tackles were flying in and after twenty minutes, Ossie somehow managed to floor David Harvey in the Leeds goal. Peter Lorimer deputised but it had an obvious detrimental effect on Leeds' performance. We eventually ran out comfortable victors and I scored twice in a 4–0 win. It was the best possible start to the new campaign, both for the team and for me personally. I managed to keep my place for the next few matches, scoring another against Leicester and another brace against Derby County. I'd scored five goals in three matches, topping the goal-scoring charts and Dave Sexton was quoted as saying, 'This is probably the finest start to a season since I took over.' Peter Osgood made it clear at the time that I should enjoy it while it lasted, because he was the only goal scorer at Chelsea – and he was right! The difference between that Chelsea team being a good team and a great team was consistency and unfortunately our form was patchy again throughout the season. We were in danger of becoming known as a decent cup side as we reached the Sixth Round of the FA Cup only losing out in a replay to a good Arsenal side. In addition, we reached the Semi-Finals of the League Cup, disappointingly losing to Norwich City over two legs. The problem was week-in, week-out consistency and we ended the season in twelfth place, Chelsea's lowest finish for ten years. I ended up being top goal-scorer with Ossie with eleven league goals, which, while I was pleased, really summed up our lack of fire in front of goal.

Off the field things were settled and Trish and I had a new addition to the family after she gave birth to Ryan. At Chelsea, things were very different and in some cases, the harmony between players and staff had turned to resentment. Despite the unrest, Chelsea arranged a three-week tour to Australia. I was particularly looking forward to this after my experience with the FA tour and the friends I had made down-under. The uncomfortable atmosphere around the camp was made worse by the fact that several players' contracts were up at the end of that season. Unbelievably, Dave Sexton thought it would be a good idea to renegotiate their contracts on the eleven-hour flight to Australia. There were bits of paper going up and down the aeroplane and the club physiotherapist, Harry Medhurst, was acting as the go-between. A piece of paper would be sent by Sexton through Medhurst with the length of the contract and how much you had been offered. If you agreed with the terms on 'the piece of paper', the player had to sign it and send it back via Medhurst. There were some major squad members involved and the fact that Dave wanted to conduct business during a flight didn't go down too well. Many of the players involved just laughed at the suggestion that a new contract would be thrashed out on the way to Australia. Don't get me wrong, Dave Sexton was a fantastic coach and a great manager, one of the best, but at that time he still had a lot to learn in terms of man-management of players off the field.

The first game was in Darwin and we had two days to prepare and get used to the high humidity. Before the match we put all our valuables into a big bag for security and the physio looked after it until after the game. We won 3–0, but when it came to collecting our valuables, Micky Droy and I were the last two out of the bath. There were no watches, no jewellery and no money left. Someone had obviously taken more than they should have. Micky, who was a big lad, stormed into the bar and said that if the money and valuables weren't in the hotel locker by the time we got back, there would be problems. Funnily enough, when we arrived back to the hotel, someone had crept back and left all our money and jewellery in an envelope. Although we had a hunch who it was, we never found out for sure. You just don't expect that from your team-mates. We then travelled to Perth and beat them 2–1 before moving on to Sydney. We had five days there and so long as we behaved ourselves and were in at a reasonable hour, had free time to explore the city prior to the game. When I say a reasonable hour, I mean about eleven o'clock. On one occasion, after a nice meal in the centre of town, Tommy and Charlie went missing again. Tommy reckoned he got in at about 2am and by-passed Ron Suart who was waiting up for them. We didn't see Charlie until the following morning when he turned up for training in a tracksuit and balaclava. Dave got all the lads together and told Charlie to take off his balaclava and shirt. He did so to reveal a battered face and knife lacerations all over his body. It was apparently the result of an altercation in a nightclub.

The following day we were due to play our final match of the tour. When Dave announced the team, Charlie's name was on the list – to the surprise of everyone. I was substitute that night and it was terrible to watch him running around clueless. He couldn't see out of his badly bruised eyes and I think Dave put him through that to teach him a lesson in front of his mates. Whether it worked or not is debatable.

After two fairly successful tours to Germany and Holland, and then Spain prior to the beginning of the 1973–74 season, I was hoping that the discontent – and the rumours about players leaving – would evaporate and we would have a decent season. By the end of August, however, we were bottom of the First Division after losing our opening three fixtures. Things picked up in November and December with a run of wins, largely down to Ossie's goals, but despite our crawling up to mid-table, the arguments between players and management continued. After we lost 4–2 at West Ham, throwing away a 2–0 lead, Dave dropped Peter Osgood, Alan Hudson, Peter Bonetti and Tommy Baldwin for the New Year's Day fixture with Sheffield United. We won the match, but shortly afterwards the problems really kicked off, with Alan and Ossie both handing in transfer requests. Alan Hudson had indeed played his last match for

Chelsea and signed for Stoke City for £240,000. Despite our relatively poor form and lowly position in the table, the league was incredibly tight and we were only seven points off third-placed Derby County as we moved into March. Tommy Baldwin had joined Ossie on the transfer list and Sexton and the board were adamant that their decision to leave Peter out of the side was for the good of the club, which was somewhat debatable considering our record in front of goal. Our cup form had also deserted us, as we fell at the first hurdles in the FA Cup Third Round to QPR and in the League Cup Second Round to our old adversaries Stoke City. The Osgood saga finally reached a head as we approached transfer deadline day and Ossie was sold to Southampton for £275,000. With those two influential players leaving, it really felt that the Chelsea I had joined was breaking up.

If you lose your best players at any standard, let alone in the First Division, you're going to struggle. Our results had taken a downturn and instead of looking at a place in the UEFA Cup, we were now concentrating on avoiding relegation. Over Easter, we picked up a win at Tottenham and a draw at Southampton which helped to consolidate our position above the bottom three and more or less guaranteed our survival. Ironically, Osgood's Southampton filled the third relegation place above Manchester United and Norwich City who also dropped into Division Two. The exodus didn't stop there. In the summer, Dave Webb signed for QPR for £100,000 and Eddie McCreadie announced his retirement. The club seemed to be crumbling around me and players were becoming increasingly disillusioned.

Even with a few fresh faces to fill the void left by Osgood and Hudson, the mood around the ground was noticeably subdued. Not even the opening of the new East Stand could raise the optimism. Our start to the season was even worse than the previous year, and we found ourselves in the relegation zone again after winning only two of our first ten games. Following the upheaval of the last season, Dave Sexton was under increasing pressure to turn the situation around from both the fans and the board of directors. The turnaround never happened and he was sacked at the beginning of October. Sexton's former assistant, Ron Suart, took over in temporary charge. I scored both Chelsea goals in a 2–1 win over Arsenal at Highbury over Christmas, adding further strings to my bow in my attempt to remain in the team. They were vital goals and an important win to help the cause as we fought to avoid being sucked into a relegation battle for the second consecutive year. We moved into February in more positive mood after a string of improved results and performances, but the form didn't last and shortly after we were knocked out of the FA Cup by Birmingham City, Suart was replaced by Eddie McCreadie who was promoted from first-team coach. With relegation looming and money extremely tight at Chelsea, further changes were afoot. Little did I know at the time that, after four seasons in west London, my time with Chelsea was coming to an end.

CHAPTER FOUR

PUNCH-UPS AND KEEP-UPS

From a personal perspective, the exodus at Chelsea in the months leading up to what was my final season in London was extremely disappointing. I felt as though I had finally been accepted by the players and the supporters, was scoring goals and playing well. The discontent between the management and some of the senior players, like Peter Osgood, Alan Hudson and Dave Webb, had been evident internally for a while, but it was still an unfortunate state of affairs when the club struggled on and off the pitch as a consequence. Eddie McCreadie was a nice guy and walked into the managerial hot-seat at Stamford Bridge in what was really a no-win situation. The expectation of the fans and the media was such after the minor successes and the failures of the 1970s, that nothing short of silverware was now acceptable. The whole mood of the club had changed.

A couple of days into his new role, Eddie pulled me aside after training to talk over my situation at Chelsea. 'Look Chris,' he started, 'I really don't want to sell you, but we have had a bid of £100,000 from Leicester City and I wondered what you thought of it.' Looking around the ground that day, thinking of the players who had departed, the now unfamiliar faces that greeted me in the morning and the shell of the club I had joined some three years earlier, even if I didn't know it at the time my mind must have been made up. Despite Eddie doing his best to keep me at the Bridge for the remainder of the 1974–75 season, it was an opportunity to move away from London, return to rural surroundings and a more family-orientated club. Eddie was absolutely brilliant, but I told him my mind was made up. He wished me luck and I made my way north to Leicester to hold talks with manager Jimmy Bloomfield.

At the time, many people in the media and friends of mine thought that moving to Leicester City was a strange move for a player who, at 25, was approaching his supposed prime. The truth of the matter was that I had never felt really settled in London. As a consequence, Trish, despite liking London, felt unsettled too, which had a knock-on effect on Adam and Ryan who were now three and eighteen months. I – no, we – needed stability away from the big city and I loved the feel of Leicester almost immediately. It was similar to Bristol, with people of a like mind. I felt happier in my own heart. In footballing terms, Leicester were struggling at the foot of Division One and whilst Chelsea were certainly not safe from relegation, Leicester's plight seemed far worse. I studied the playing staff at Filbert Street and really couldn't understand why they were in their current situation. They had quality players in their line-up like Keith Weller, Steve Whitworth, Jon Sammels, Dennis Rofe, Jeff Blockley, Alan Birchenall and Frank Worthington. How on earth were they in this sort of relegation trouble? The talks with Jimmy Bloomfield went well and he seemed a nice, genuine man, but once again I fell for the same old flannel! My one regret was not speaking to the other club interested in getting my signature.

Everton had matched Leicester's offer while I was having talks with Jimmy. I was in Leicester for two days and in hindsight I should have spoken to Everton as well, if not purely to see what they were offering, then to go for the experience. They were a massive club. The worst that could have happened was that I would have returned to Leicester with a stronger negotiating hand. Jimmy Bloomfield, however, was very convincing. I didn't speak to Everton and I signed for Leicester City. The first man I met on leaving the manager's office that day was a guy called Lennie Glover. He was a hero with the fans, who had been with the club most of his life, but no longer a regular in the starting eleven. There were no pleasantries and I will never forget what he said to me. 'You've made the biggest mistake of your life!' Great, I thought, some family club and this is the guy the fans worship! I realised then and in the days that followed that in many ways Leicester had similar traits to Chelsea and potentially some of the same problems. There were certain cliques and groups that had existed at Filbert Street for so long that I was never going to be a part of them. It didn't really bother me. I had been through similar treatment at Chelsea but on a much larger scale. I felt more confident, not only in my footballing ability, but also how to handle myself off the pitch. At Chelsea I had to grow-up fast and, in the words of Dave Sexton, 'learn even faster'. I could now put my west London education into practice but this time with the backing of a settled family life, in surroundings in which I felt comfortable. Lennie's comments certainly made me think, but the words didn't worry me as much as they might have done some three or four years previously. His welcoming words of wisdom smacked of the bitterness of a one-time hero. I had signed for Leicester City and deep down I knew that it was the right move.

My first few weeks in Leicester were spent in the Posthouse Hotel just outside the city. I stayed there for about two months, until the end of the season, when Trish and I had more time to look for a house of our own. It wasn't the best hotel and I missed my family. In fact the only thing it was good for was getting a few of the lads back for a drink, all on the bill. With the end of the season looming, important games were coming thick and fast and the priority was to get ourselves out of the First Division relegation zone. When I left Stamford Bridge, Chelsea were ten points ahead of Leicester with ten games of the season to play, hence the comments on my departure. I will never forget my debut for Leicester, away to Coventry City. In my haste to sign and get relatively settled in Leicester, I had even left my boots at Chelsea. Thankfully the club had them collected and delivered to me in time for the match on the Saturday. I was looking forward to the Coventry game for three reasons. The first was that I was obviously keen to make a good impression in front of the fans and the second was because of my previous record at Highfield Road. In the three games I had played there, we had won two and drawn one, and I had scored in two out of the three fixtures. The third reason was because it meant that I would face my 'old pal' and ex-Bristol Rovers player Larry Lloyd again. He didn't like playing against me for some strange reason, despite my being a little flyweight and his being a fifteen-stone giant. Maybe it was because I had more hair, but then again, back then I probably had more hair than most people. The game itself went extremely well, both for me and the team. The 2–2 score-line doesn't really tell how well we played. We dictated large spells of the match, passed the ball around well and if it wasn't for a late goal being disallowed in somewhat debatable circumstances we could have taken all the points.

Nevertheless, in our situation you always took what you could get, and goals from Bob Lee and Frank Worthington gave us the point that meant that Leicester moved out of the relegation zone for the first time that season.

Our next fixture was against Liverpool at home in midweek and we drew again, this time 1–1 being the score-line. It could be argued that this wasn't the best of starts, but we were getting points on the board in tough games. As with many changes in football, everything happens so fast that you can't take everything in. I realised that, after the Coventry and Liverpool games, I still hadn't really got to know many of the lads yet. Playing in a match is getting to know someone on one level, but it really helps on the pitch if you also know them better socially. As with Chelsea and Bristol City, Leicester City had a players' room where staff and their families could go for a drink after the match. I did just this after the Liverpool game and was subsequently invited to go with a few of the lads for a meal in the city centre. A Leicester City fanatic owned the restaurant and he would welcome the players after a home game, so they could have a bit of fun and relax in familiar surroundings. It sounded similar to our frequent visits to Alexander's at Chelsea and, as I didn't really fancy going back to a lifeless hotel room on my own, I saw it as a good opportunity to get to know my new team mates. The night was going well and listening to my instincts about the club and the city appeared to be paying dividends. Unfortunately towards the end of the night things turned a little sour. Alan Birchenall was a great lad, but after a few too many drinks could get a bit aggressive. He accused me of making advances towards his wife and we nearly ended up scrapping in the restaurant. The rest of the players knew what he could get like and told me not to worry as he had made that particular accusation about most of them at one time or another. Even though Alan was clearly in the wrong on this occasion, I still didn't really want the aggravation and unrest that such an incident causes after just one week in Leicester. As it turned out, Alan and I became good friends and soon after we even moved in next door to him in Coalville, to a beautiful four-bedroom house in a friendly area.

After the previous draws against Coventry and Liverpool, we were now under pressure to collect maximum points in order to consolidate and extend our position outside the relegation zone. Wolves, whom we played at home the following Saturday, were still on a high after their 7–1 thrashing of Chelsea the previous week. When I left Chelsea, they were relatively comfortable and half way up the league but a couple of bad results had dragged them into the dog-fight at the bottom. Suddenly the unthinkable was becoming a possibility for

Chelsea. We beat Wolves 3–2 and I scored a hat-trick, the winner coming in the last minute. It wasn't the best hat-trick you will ever see and scrappy to say the least, but a win is a win and a hat-trick is a hat-trick. The morning's newspapers were full of it and I also got man-of-the-match, which really put the icing on the cake. My performance against Wolves had really kick-started my run of form for Leicester. I scored twice in a 3–0 home victory against West Ham United and a late equaliser against Leeds United in a 2–2 draw at Elland Road. I then scored another brace in a 4–0 win at home to Newcastle – Leicester's biggest win of the season. I was also given another man-of-the-match award and Frank Worthington gave me a bouquet of flowers to mark my performance. A little tongue in cheek, I suspect! It was certainly a purple patch and Frank was probably right in that everything I touched at that time seemed to end up in the back of the net. I had scored eight goals in seven games since my arrival and together we had lifted Leicester City out of the relegation zone to safety. In addition, Chelsea were one of only four teams still fighting for survival, and whilst it may have appeared strange at the time, my move with ten games to go was turning out to be a shrewd option, both for me and my new employers. By the end of the season, I was a local hero with the fans, and Leicester City had survived in Division One by three clear points. Chelsea drew their final two matches of the season against Sheffield United and Everton, who both finished in the top six, and were relegated along with Carlisle United and Luton Town. The 'glory days', or maybe more appropriately, the 'glory nights' of the 1960s and early 1970s, were now over at Stamford Bridge.

It was the best possible start at a new club for me. Jimmy Bloomfield was quoted as saying that, 'Chris was the best signing I ever made,' which was quite a compliment when you think about how many players he had signed – and who they were. On this occasion, whilst I considered myself to be playing well, it was all about the goals and the timing of my arrival. I had made an impression, but the following season would be a new campaign completely, starting from scratch and proving that I wasn't just a ten-game wonder. Chelsea's disastrous situation saw further players leaving the club. Luckily for Leicester and for me personally, my old mate Steve Kember arrived at Filbert Street. There was already a strong London presence amongst the players at Leicester, with the likes of Keith Weller and Dennis Rofe, so Steve must have felt right at home. There was a nice mix of players and quite a few local lads who were particularly passionate about the club. There was one thing that we all had in common, whether from Leicester, London or Bristol. We wanted Leicester to succeed and were desperate for the new season to start.

On arriving back after our brief summer break, training was, as always, tough but much needed and we embarked on a pre-season tour of Sweden in good spirits. The tour was purely focussed on football and was a far cry from the Chelsea trips abroad I had experienced. We won all our games in Sweden against First and Second Division clubs and continued our run when on home soil. We won all our twelve pre-season friendlies, which was fantastic for confidence, but also had a down-side. We had a terrible start to the 1975–76 season proper and after six league games we hadn't managed to put a win on the board. I started the season competing for a place in the Leicester attack with Frank Worthington and Bob Lee. Frank was an automatic choice, which was fair enough because he was a lovely man, a terrific footballer and was adored by the fans. When I played with the likes of Frank, John Galley at Bristol City and, to a certain extent, Ossie at Chelsea, I could feed off them. Frank, however, was a different talent altogether and didn't like to do the simple things. You could also kick Frank around the pitch all afternoon and he wouldn't retaliate, whereas Ossie gave as good as he got. It is debatable as to which is the better characteristic, but somewhere in between would be my preferred option. During the Newcastle fixture at Filbert Street towards the end of the previous season, we were 3–0 up with about ten minutes to go. Frank received the ball by the enclosure next to the tunnel and juggled the ball six or seven times, flicked it onto his head and then volleyed the ball over the stand. The players couldn't believe what was going on, but the fans loved it, they loved him and his showmanship. You can imagine what the Newcastle players were thinking and yes, he was taking the piss, but certainly from our perspective, nobody really cared. That was Frank after all, but our poor start to the new campaign led to Jimmy Bloomfield panicking and making changes around the pitch, including in attack. Jimmy started by playing Frank and me, but then tried Frank and Bob for a number of games. One of the reasons early on for the changes was my own fault. Twenty-two minutes into our first game of the season at home to Birmingham, I was sent off after a punch-up with Birmingham's John Roberts. I then returned to the side, but struggled in comparison to the end of the last season, scoring only two goals in twelve games. I was dropped and didn't complain, despite seemingly being made a scapegoat for the team's failings. In certain games, I was asked to drop into midfield and carry out a marking role, when I knew – and Jimmy knew – that playing as a striker was my strongest position. Despite being regarded as not a goal-scoring centre-forward in some critic's eyes, I personally thought that, during my career, I often scored important goals against top opposition and I completed an unusual hat-trick during that season. Having scored a hat-trick for Chelsea in the League Cup before my departure and a hat-trick against Wolves for Leicester on my arrival in the Midlands, I completed the set with an FA Cup Third Round hat-trick against Sheffield United in a 3–0 win in the January. I was told at the time that I was one of only five players who had achieved the feat of scoring a hat-trick in the League, the League Cup and the FA Cup in a twelve-month period. It is an achievement of which I am still proud today. I classed myself as a hard-working team player but still scored goals – unfortunately not enough, some would say. At Chelsea we had a chart which listed players' assists in the three passes which led directly towards a goal. I frequently appeared on this chart and classed this as an area which was as vital as scoring myself. The hat-trick of hat-tricks helped to prove that I could, and in fact did, score goals. Thankfully things also improved for the team and at one point we looked as though we could be pushing for a UEFA Cup place. Unfortunately we just missed out in seventh spot, but after the start we made to the season, a top-seven finish was more than acceptable.

I was beginning to realise that a pattern was emerging at Leicester. A good pre-season, some encouraging results and great performances, albeit in friendly matches, all meant nothing when the season began. Again, we started the 76–77 season relatively poorly and my late equaliser in a 2–2 draw at QPR in September gave us our sixth successive draw. It was disappointing, because I was looking forward to the new season for two reasons. First of all I was keen to build on our improved performances at the back end of the last season and secondly, because Bristol City would be one of our opponents, having won promotion from Division Two. Despite moving to Chelsea and subsequently Leicester City, I had always been and always will be a Bristol City supporter and was celebrating like any fan when they finally achieved Division One status after a 1–0 win against

Portsmouth at Ashton Gate. If City had been in Division One five
years earlier, I know that I would never have left Ashton Gate.
However, I had never regretted leaving my favourite club when I did
and whilst I was eagerly looking forward to playing against some of
my old mates for the first time since departing, it was frustrating when
things weren't going well at Leicester.

When the Bristol City fixture finally came around, there was a lot
of coverage in the local press in both Leicester and Bristol, as well as
in the national papers, about my first competitive return to Ashton
Gate. The Robins had had a mixed start, winning away to Arsenal on
the opening day of the season, only to lose their leading striker Paul
Cheesley with a serious knee injury in their first home game. After
four games, Bristol City were undefeated in fourth place, but had hit
a rocky spell by the time Leicester were the visitors. It was a strange
feeling going back to Bristol to play against City and if I was
completely honest, when it came to it, I wasn't that keen on playing.
I would have hated to have scored. Nevertheless, I couldn't wait to
play against my old mate Geoff Merrick, with whom I had grown up
in Bedminster. Unfortunately, Geoff twisted his ankle half way
through the match and had to be replaced. Fortunately for Leicester,
Keith Weller was having one of his many brilliant games and
completely dominated the match. He scored the only goal of the game
and we came away with maximum points. After everything that had
happened, I still received a tremendous welcome from the crowd.

When things aren't going well on the pitch, incidents tend to occur
on the training ground. Jeff Blockley was a strapping central defender
who had signed for Leicester shortly before I made my move from
Chelsea. While I may have scored the goals, Jeff's arrival certainly
helped to hold together the defensive aspect of our game. Maybe it
was because of our recent performances, but training in mid-October
1976 was getting very competitive and five-a-sides were just as lively.
A few nasty tackles were flying around the gym and Jeff was looking
to sort out one or two of the young apprentices, which I didn't think
was appropriate. After one tackle on a youngster, I thought he had
overstepped the mark and I took an almighty swipe at him. I knew it
wasn't the right thing to do, but in the heat of the moment, I put
myself in the position of the apprentice and acted accordingly. My
punch landed right on his cheek bone. I have never heard such a noise
in all of my life and the whole training session stopped as everyone

looked over to see what had happened. The rest of the lads jumped in as if to split us up, which was pointless as Jeff couldn't move on the ground with his cheek bone completely broken. Jimmy Bloomfield stepped in and told us to get into his office immediately, which was impossible for Jeff as he just wanted to get to the hospital. Consequently, George, our physiotherapist, took Jeff to the hospital and I made my way to see the manager. The thing that I couldn't understand was that Jimmy had watched the situation escalate from the sidelines and said nothing. That was Jimmy, he liked to see a bit of passion and wound players up accordingly, but on this occasion it had seriously backfired. To be honest it was the last thing the club needed as we were already struggling in the centre-half department and now we would be without another defender for the best part of two months. Unfortunately the incident made the local and national newspapers. Someone at the club had let the story out and it was the headline on the back of the *Daily Mirror*, although they said it was an elbow that had caused the damage in a 'training ground collision'. Jimmy swore that he didn't see the incident and we both escaped any kind of punishment. It is fair to say that Jeff's wife wasn't too pleased with that outcome. We had a club party on the Saturday and she came up to me and made her feelings clear. I stood there and took her verbal onslaught, after all what else could I do? I didn't mean to do it, well, not break his cheek bone anyway, but I was in the wrong.

Our performances didn't improve on the pitch and by November, I was becoming increasingly unsettled. I was ready to go home to Bristol. I had put in three transfer requests before, finally, the fourth was accepted. There had been some speculation in the press in the run-up to my decision, but I certainly didn't generate the articles written. While Jimmy was reluctant to sell me, I think he knew that my heart was no longer at Leicester City. I had received a couple of phone calls and knew that Bristol City were interested and, more importantly, had the £110,000 asking price to re-sign me. With pressure building at Leicester, Jimmy Bloomfield was sacked just as my transfer to Bristol City was going through. He was replaced by Frank McLintock, who later told me that he tried his best to get hold of me to convince me to stay. I told him, there was nothing he could have said or done to persuade me not to sign for Bristol City. He understood. My only concern about a move back to Bristol was the contract negotiations. Bristol City had spent quite heavily on strengthening the squad in preparation for survival. I was determined not repeat my mistakes of the past. I had signed for Leicester City eighteen months ago on £125-a-week and knew that a rise in salary was due. Sure enough, my heart over-ruled my head and I signed for Bristol City for exactly the same money – £125-a-week. I don't think that money back then was as important to players as it is today, but I did kick myself. I even missed out on my cut of the transfer fee from when I moved from Chelsea to Leicester. I was legally entitled to five per cent of the fee, which equated to around £5,000. I missed out despite Bristol City manager Alan Dicks saying he would try to get it back for me. I never saw a penny. It was a similar situation to the one I faced at Chelsea whereby I still had time to run on my contract and because my share of the transfer fee was spread over the term of my contract, I ended up losing out. Alan had his job to do for the club and signing for the same money was my own fault, but I was that keen to bring my family back to Bristol. Whilst City letting me know their interest in me before Leicester City were officially aware wasn't completely above board, I can honestly say that I have never accepted a 'back-hander' in my life. I always put football and integrity before money.

I had a genuinely happy eighteen months in Leicester. It was and still is a great city, with fantastic people and a terrific football club, but my desire to return to my roots and the football club I loved was simply too strong. Now that my head and heart were focussed, I couldn't think of anything else apart from pulling on the red jersey once more and keeping Bristol City in the one place I had always dreamed both they and I would be – the top-flight of English football.

CHAPTER FIVE

MOVING DOWN ... STAYING UP

My transfer from Leicester City to Bristol City took just under one month to complete, and during that time media speculation was rife. Peter Godsiff, a well-known and highly regarded sports journalist in Bristol, whom I had known for many years, had telephoned me the week before I signed to tell me that Bristol City had tabled a bid for me and he asked if I would be interested. I was over the moon that an offer had finally arrived. The thought of fulfilling another of my ambitions, to play for City in the top-flight, sent a tingle down my spine. My mother, Grace, had a slightly different view. She thought I was mad to return to City and told the local press in no uncertain terms. I was disappointed to read it in the *Green 'Un* (the local weekend sports paper in Bristol) even angry at first, but I knew she only had my best interests at heart. After all, I think she loved the Leicester area and lifestyle as much as I did, on her frequent visits with my father.

City manager Alan Dicks contacted me to arrange a meeting. He asked if I could meet him at noon the following day at the Posthouse Hotel on the outskirts of Leicester, a place I knew only too well from my initial stay some eighteen months earlier. I met Alan and his secretary the next day and we agreed a contract that would take me back to Ashton Gate. The first thing Alan said as we sat down was, 'Sorry Chris, but I haven't got any money. We used up any spare cash when we signed Norman Hunter and Peter Cormack.' Norman signed in October 1976 and Peter had been signed a month later. Here I was, signing in December and once again Chris Garland had missed the gravy boat – or so I was told! Once again, money wasn't particularly high on my priority list and I trusted what Alan had told me. The only money I was determined to retain was my cut of the signing-on fee from when I signed for Leicester. Despite Alan's efforts, the money never materialised. I had signed for the same weekly wage as I was on at Leicester City, with lower bonuses and I even had to pay for my own removals when we moved south. For me, everything was about playing football, and playing football for Bristol City.

My first match on returning to Bristol was on Tuesday 30 November 1976, playing in Trevor Tainton's testimonial match at Ashton Gate against Bristol Rovers. It was unusual to have a testimonial in the middle of the season, but I looked upon it as an opportunity to get to know the players and surroundings once again. In the five-and-a-half years since my departure, the ground itself hadn't really changed, but personnel at 'The Gate' certainly had. Twentieth of April 1976 is a very special date for Bristol City supporters, because after ten years in Division Two and sixty-five years outside the top-flight, City had won promotion to the First Division. On this particular occasion, it certainly was fair to say that *Bristol* City had won promotion. Of the regular starting eleven, six were Bristolian and no fewer than seven had progressed from the youth ranks. In my eyes, the players who achieved the dream of so many fans – and I count myself as a fan – deserve a special acknowledgement. The appearances during that special 1975/76 season were (goals in brackets): Ray Cashley 42, Gerry Gow 42 (5), Geoff Merrick 42 (2), Trevor Tainton 42, Tom Richie 42 (18), Gary Collier 40 (1), Brian Drysdale 39, Paul Cheesley 38 (15), Gerry Sweeney 32 (5), Jimmy Mann 30 (7), Donnie Gillies 22 (1), Clive Whitehead 19 (4), Mike Brolly 14 (1), Keith Fear 13, John Emanuel 3, Steve Harding 2.

Rarely had a youth policy produced as fruitful a set of players as the one set up by Alan Dicks a decade earlier. Individuals, as well as the club itself, had seen the benefits, myself included, but now it was clear for all to see. Many players from the promotion squad were still in the side and I knew several of them, either from playing together as youngsters or from my initial time with the club, which made settling in again a lot easier. However, there were also a few new faces, like Norman Hunter from Leeds United and Peter Cormack from Liverpool, both of whom I had played against, to add experience and strength to the squad.

Trevor's testimonial was fully deserved because his commitment to Bristol City since signing for the Robins as an apprentice in 1965 was second-to-none. A local lad, product of the youth system, talented footballer and all-round lovely man, Trevor epitomised what Bristol City was all about. The fact that the match was against Bristol Rovers made it all the more special. As I'd come to expect over the years against our local rivals, the game was comfortable in front of a decent crowd and I managed to score both goals in a 2–1 win to help reacquaint myself with the supporters.

My first competitive match back in a red shirt was the following Saturday, when we hosted Leeds United at Ashton Gate. I was nervous as City were in a precarious position towards the bottom of the table, but also keen to help move them clear of the relegation zone. The press were going crazy at my return, with some predicting I would add five-thousand fans on to the total gate. I wasn't sure about that, but my move had certainly generated a lot of interest in the local and national media. The training sessions between Trevor's testimonial match and the Leeds fixture simply flew by and before I knew it, the game was upon me. I met the rest of the players and staff at Ashton Court Country Club, later to be known as Redwood Lodge Hotel and Country Club, which is three or four miles from Ashton Gate. Alan preferred that we met away from the ground, even for home games. That way, we could have our pre-match meal and chat in relative privacy. I usually had a steak or beans on toast, depending on my mood or nerves. We had a meeting at one o'clock to discuss the forthcoming game and then made our way to the ground. It was a beautifully sunny December day and during the short journey to the ground, I felt the nerves disappear and was now really looking forward to the match.

As we drove down the hill past the entrance to the Ashton Court Estate towards the Clanage, where I had played football as a youngster, we hit thick fog. You really did struggle to see further than ten feet in front of your face. We managed to get to the ground and park the cars, but if anything the weather was getting worse. Unbelievably the gates and turnstiles were open and supporters were being admitted to the terraces. I honestly couldn't see how this match was going to proceed. With about ten minutes until kick-off, just over 30,000 supporters had packed into Ashton Gate. I believe you are supposed to be able to see the goalposts from the half-way line, but on this occasion there was no chance of seeing the eighteen-yard box, let alone the back of the net. Surprisingly, the referee decided to start the game which, after the build up, was a relief for me in many ways. I'm sure the fans were just as relieved, but exactly how much they saw of the match, I really don't know.

As the game went on, the fog worsened. Mid-way through the first half, I managed to get my head to a corner and hit the crossbar, but I'm the first to admit that it was certainly more luck than judgement. As I was the only one to have seen it, I told everyone that I had out-jumped three defenders and that it was a fantastic header. Nobody could really argue with me, despite the fact that all I had done was thrown myself into fresh air!

We went in at half-time all square at 0–0, but the match itself was ridiculous. The two managers met with the referee during the break and decided that the game should be abandoned. It was a great disappointment to the 31,000 strong crowd, not to mention an anti-climax to me, but it really was the only sensible option. Incidentally, Leicester City lost 6–2 against Birmingham City in their first game after my departure. It is purely coincidental, of course, but interesting on top of Chelsea's 7–1 hammering in their next match after I had left west London.

Paul Cheesley, still having problems with his knee injury, was missing from the team. At that time, the true severity of his injury hadn't been fully diagnosed. In hindsight, maybe too much was expected of Paul too soon, which ultimately had a massive detrimental effect on his career. A.D. had signed me with a view to playing alongside Paul, with him being close to my ideal playing partner – tall, strong, good in the air as well as on the ground, and he could also score goals. Paul was similar in many ways to my hero, John Atyeo. Consequently, it was a great frustration and one of my own personal regrets that we never had the chance to realise our potential as a strike duo.

Alan was also devastated. The plan was for me to play alongside Paul, with Tom Ritchie, another of the promotion heroes, dropping back into midfield. In Paul's absence, we only had three recognised strikers, but in myself, Tom Ritchie and Keith Fear, we didn't have a true centre-forward. As a result, I was thrust into the role, despite being far from the ideal build for a true centre-forward in the top division in England. It wasn't really my game. I wasn't a target man, but suddenly I had players trying to feed off me instead of the other way around. You could see almost immediately that we were going to struggle – and we did.

It took me almost two months to score my first goal and after the build-up to the abandoned Leeds United fixture, I was under pressure from the fans and the media. Things were getting desperate and we needed results fast as we were now in dire straits at the bottom of the league. I scored against Newcastle United in a 1–1 draw at Ashton Gate in early February and followed that up a couple of weeks later with the winning goal against championship-chasers Manchester City in a 1–0 home win. But there was little doubt in my mind that playing centre-forward had affected my confidence. The fans were getting on my back, which was understandable as the club had paid £110,000 for me and I wasn't producing the performances, but it wasn't through lack of effort. I accepted that it wasn't good enough and even had meetings with Alan Dicks to discuss the possibility of trying either Tom or Keith in the position, but at the same time it would have looked bad for Alan with the directors if he dropped me. As a fan of the club it broke my heart to have some supporters on my back, as I always gave 100% and was maybe trying too hard. In fact, I was very lucky with the fans at Ashton Gate even when things weren't going so well. I received criticism from some sections and I did deserve it at times, but I had a core set of supporters in the enclosure, just below the main grandstand, who cheered me whatever my performance. I think they always knew that I would never want to let Bristol City down.

Eventually the pressure of playing in an unfamiliar position got too much, reaching the point where I virtually asked A.D. to drop me. Tom Ritchie was subsequently given the role. I was substitute for a number of matches, playing a bit part in some games. It was a surprise to me, and the media, when Alan recalled me for the visit of Tottenham Hotspur in mid-April. We picked up a 1–0 win thanks to a goal from Peter Cormack and over the coming weeks, I regained some much-needed match fitness. Alan must have known something that I didn't, as without these games I simply wouldn't have been a viable option for the run-in.

Unfortunately our results didn't pick up enough, as we collected only five points from a possible ten following my return to the starting line-up. With five games to go we had Manchester United, Leeds United and Liverpool at home and Middlesbrough and Coventry City away. Back then it was still two points for a win and to stand a realistic chance of First Division survival, Alan set us a target of seven out of eight points. Despite our bad run of results, the one saving grace was that other clubs at the bottom had performed equally poorly over the period. It was extremely tight at the foot of the table, with

Tottenham Hotspur, Stoke City, Sunderland, West Ham United and Coventry City all perilously close to the drop. On current form, the remaining five fixtures wouldn't have been our choice of matches to play in order to stay up. Nevertheless, they were and it was up to the players to produce.

Ashton Gate was packed to the rafters for the visit of Manchester United and the electric atmosphere in the stands transferred to the players on the pitch. I notched the equalising goal, ironically my first since scoring against Manchester City in February, to earn us a vital point and give the players and supporters renewed confidence. The last thing we needed at this stage was another tough match, but Leeds United were the visitors only three days later. The fans could sense that survival was now a distinct possibility. I scored the only goal of the game with a left-footed drive from twelve yards in the sixty-ninth minute to earn us two vital points. Not only did we win, but we dominated large spells of the game. Had it not been for an outstanding display of goalkeeping by David Stewart in the Leeds goal, the end result could have been far more convincing. It was by far my best game since returning to Bristol. Maybe Alan had looked at what I had achieved at Leicester City when I arrived in the Midlands in helping them stay up and thought it was an omen.

I took a knock in the Leeds game which remained sore for the rest of the week, meaning that I missed training. I knew it wasn't serious, but it was sore and the best way I could describe it was like having toothache in my leg. Having hit a rich vein of much-needed form, I was devastated to miss the following game away at Middlesbrough on the Saturday, but the rest of the lads pulled out the stops to pick up another point in a goal-less draw. With two games to go, our situation still looked less than favourable, despite an upturn in performances and results. Stoke City and Tottenham both dropped points, but we still needed three points from the remaining matches against Liverpool and Coventry to stay up.

City's biggest crowd of the season of 38,698 turned up just two days after the Middlesbrough game on the evening of Monday 16 May to watch us battle with the Merseysiders. It really seemed as though everybody I knew from the city had turned up. Liverpool, who had a fantastic team, had been crowned League champions and arrived in Bristol off the back of an eighteen-match unbeaten run, but expectations in Bristol were still high. Even though the League title had been sewn up, Liverpool still put out their strongest eleven in a bid to extend their run. As for us, everyone in the camp was confident and we felt you could have sent us out to play any team in the world that night and we would have beaten them. I went into the game full of confidence and couldn't see us losing.

We had a reality check after half-an-hour, when David Johnson headed home a Phil Neal cross. We looked nervous at the back and in possession of the ball, but with just three minutes to go until the interval, we equalised. Clive Whitehead, who had been in tremendous form terrorising defences, went on a mazy run and chipped in a cross from the right wing and I met his centre with a diving header which flew past Ray Clemence. Ashton Gate erupted. I looked round at the players and the staff and saw passion and hunger in their eyes. There was no way we were going to lose this game. When we walked into the dressing room at half-time, the tension had turned to excitement. Coach John Sillett, who had been known to have the odd flutter in his time, was shouting and bawling at everyone as he usually does, telling us how much money he had on us to stay up and if we lost the match how he'd be skint for the rest of his life. However, with the exception of John, the air was strangely relaxed but focussed – we knew what we had to do.

We started the second half well and stepped up a gear. We looked the better side. Both Trevor Tainton and I had efforts cleared off the line and we had most of the possession, but we needed that second goal. It looked as though time could be running out and the tension was beginning to build once again around the ground.

With quarter-of-an-hour to go, Donnie Gillies sent a ball into the box at the 'Open End' of Ashton Gate, which Ray Clemence came to gather. Clemence shouted it was his ball, but mistimed his jump. I crept in between him and the brilliant Emlyn Hughes and managed to get my head on the ball and guide it into the empty net for my second goal of the game. My first thought was to run towards the fans who had supported me through thick and thin and I sprinted towards the Enclosure. I remember it extremely clearly and can still see the looks on the supporters' faces. They were going absolutely mental! I glanced towards the dug-out and saw a beaming Alan Dicks and a relieved John Sillett, who was no doubt starting to count his money. It was the most incredible feeling. We managed to hang on for the final fifteen minutes, although Liverpool did raise their game to push us to the wire.

Some sceptics commented that Liverpool weren't that interested in the match, but I'm convinced that they wanted that equaliser. You don't become true champions by letting teams at the bottom of the league beat you. True winners are winners in every situation, in every game and Liverpool had a team full of them. At the final whistle, the relief was overwhelming. We had achieved A.D.'s target of six points from four games and with other results also going our way, we now needed just one point from our final match against similarly relegation-threatened Coventry City at Highfield Road. Tiredness wasn't really a factor now, even though we had played four mentally and physically draining games in ten days. We were running on pure passion and adrenalin and as far as the players were concerned, the game couldn't come quickly enough. Fortunately, we had to wait only another three days.

The build up to the Coventry City game really was unbelievable. I wanted to go in for a massage on the Tuesday, the day after the Liverpool match, but with all the media coverage was advised to stay at home. The local news channels reported that over fifty coaches would be travelling to the Midlands from Bristol, not to mention the thousands making the journey by train and car. It really was starting to dawn on me, both as a player and supporter – the sheer magnitude of this fixture. Bristolians wanted to keep a team in the top-flight of English football. Even Rovers fans wanted City to stay up, to keep football in the West Country firmly on the map. If a particular club is doing well in a city, then the city itself does well and no doubt some of the prosperity and 'feel good factor' around the red half of Bristol had rubbed off on those in blue and white quarters. The build up to what was one of the biggest fixtures in Bristol City's long history had picked up steam and by the time the morning of the match arrived, the game dominated all areas of the media.

We left Ashton Gate and made the relatively short trip up the M5 on the morning of the match and Alan Dicks had bought in a few dozen cream cakes for the journey to make sure all the players had plenty of carbohydrates in their system. The club shop had sold out of anything that was red and white and the match had taken on the feeling of a cup final. The supporters club had run out of coaches, local travel firms reported an unprecedented demand for private hire and British Rail added an additional 'football special' rail service. Bristol City's secretary, Tony Rance, was quoted as saying that the three thousand stand tickets had been snapped up immediately by City fans, but estimated that around twelve-thousand would be making the journey. The whole of Bristol was involved. Even a judge at Bristol Crown Court decided to let a jury hearing a protracted fraud case adjourn forty minutes early so that some of those in attendance could get to the match. It really was like nothing I had experienced before.

As we travelled up the M5, there was one thing that was niggling away at me. Geoff Merrick, the club captain and rock at the heart of City's defence for years, including the promotion campaign, was missing. Back in October, Geoff reluctantly switched positions to left full-back, as A.D. made room to incorporate new signing Norman Hunter. Geoff performed admirably in the role, but missed the Liverpool victory through a niggling injury to his left ankle. Everyone assumed that Geoff would be recalled to the team for the Coventry match if fit, but despite proving his fitness, he was amazingly left out of the team. I really felt for Geoff because as well as the pressures on the pitch, he and his wife Wendy had been experiencing a testing period in their personal lives. Wendy had spent eight weeks in hospital and only returned to their home in Nailsea the day before the Coventry game, following the premature birth of twins. It put football into perspective, but nevertheless Geoff was upset, whilst the players, supporters and media were all equally shocked. Despite his obvious disappointment, Geoff drove up to Coventry, along with the thousands from Bristol to be part of the occasion and cheer us on.

We arrived in Coventry shortly before lunch and relaxed for the afternoon. We had a pre-match meal at 4.30pm and then, as usual, had a meeting to discuss tactics. Alan's right-hand man, Tony Collins, used to run through each of the opposition's players and talk through defending and attacking at corners and free-kicks. Alan would often take one look at Tony's notes, screw them up and throw them on the floor, before running through his own plans. It was a bit of an act, because Tony had spent all week putting the notes together and A.D. had obviously looked at them before and probably knew them by heart. In many cases Alan would go and watch the future opposition for himself anyway. On this occasion, the planning was meticulous and each individual player knew exactly what he had to do. When we arrived at Highfield Road, the crowds of supporters in red and white and sky blue was a sight to behold. It was a massive game for both clubs. The situation was black and white. If Sunderland managed to get at least a point against Everton, either Bristol City or Coventry City would be relegated. I looked out of the window of the coach as we approached the ground and thought, how the hell can I let these fans down? Alan Dicks and his coaching staff reiterated my own personal thoughts to us all in the run-up to kick-off. Inside the ground it was a spectacular sight for Bristol City players. It seemed as though three sides out of the four were packed with City fans. There was red and white everywhere and the atmosphere was more like a home game. The warm-up was relaxed and the air in the dressing room confident yet focussed as kick-off time approached. Alan Dicks was nowhere to be seen and the players weren't sure as to exactly what was going on. Alan returned shortly after to tell us that the game had been delayed due to crowd congestion. At the time, I didn't give it a second thought. We all waited the ten minutes or so, which seemed like hours under the circumstances and then finally made our way out into the arena.

We started well, but it was apparent from the off that Coventry's Tommy Hutchinson had decided that he was going to be the star of the show. It was as if he had a rocket up his backside. All our best-laid plans seemed to be going astray after just fifteen minutes, when Hutchinson scored to put Coventry 1–0 up. Tommy was a fantastically gifted footballer and could turn it on whenever he wanted to. Unfortunately for us, he had decided that this particular evening would be one of those times. Our efforts to pull back the deficit proved fruitless and we came off the pitch at half-time distraught. We didn't know how Sunderland were getting on, but all we did know was that if we lost this game we would be relegated. The air in the dressing room was one of disbelief. Things were not looking good. Alan and his staff did their best to lift everyone, as we prepared to play the second-half, but we all knew what we had to do and the consequences if we failed. We did step up a gear at the start of the second period. We had to. Tommy Hutchinson, however, was unrelenting and seemed to be everywhere. Because of his work rate, it wasn't a surprise to see him pop up in our penalty area seven minutes into the second-half to put Coventry 2–0 to the good. The writing was on the wall, but once again I looked around at the fans that had travelled to Coventry for us. For us! Other players must have drawn the same inspiration and within ninety seconds, Gerry Gow decided this was the right time to score his first and only goal of the season from twelve yards. Gerry was always good for at least one goal per season, but I still did a double-take when I saw him in the box. The players were visibly lifted and we gradually took control of the game. With eleven minutes to go, Gary Collier launched a free-kick into Coventry territory which I got my head to and nodded down towards Donnie Gillies. Donnie was up for the free-kick from his right-back position and thumped the ball into the corner of the net from ten yards.

The crowd went crazy, the players went mental and at that point we knew that there was only one team that was going on to win the match. We continued to dominate, but the pace of the match was still frantic. With just under ten minutes to go, the scoreboard flashed up the score from Goodison Park: Everton 2 Sunderland 0. A ripple of excitement passed around the ground as supporters realised that a draw would now be good enough to keep both Bristol City and Coventry City in Division One. There weren't many mathematical geniuses on the pitch, but fortunately it didn't take one to realise the situation. Alan Dicks and Coventry's managing director Jimmy Hill, who were close friends from Alan's days at Coventry, were shouting at the players, but all the players were already talking to each other and agreed to play keep-ball.

The remainder of the match turned into a farce as we kept possession in our own half and Coventry did little to try and win it back. All except Tommy Hutchinson that is, who was desperate for his hat-trick! Being a Jock, he wasn't best pleased when I tried to explain that both of us staying up was more important than his own personal tally. In the end his own players calmed him down and we played out the remaining minutes to the bemusement of Ron Challis, who was refereeing the match. 'Don't do anything stupid', was the shout, 'no free-kicks around the box.' Hutchinson was still falling over trying to win a free-kick in a goal-scoring position. It was a ridiculous situation, but it suited both sides. When Mr Challis blew the final whistle, it was the most fantastic feeling. The crowd flooded onto the pitch, players were lifted aloft and it took me a good twenty minutes to get to the dressing room. Not that I wanted to come off that pitch. I wanted to savour every moment. We knew we were going to have one or two drinks that night. As I was sitting in the mayhem of the dressing room, the importance of the ten-minute delay at the start of the match suddenly dawned on me. I was convinced that, having brought the score back to 2–2, we could have gone on to win the match. Everyone at the time, including me, thought that Alan was a genius to get the game delayed, but even now he stands by his account of that evening. Alan still recalls the night's events vividly:

> The Chief of Police called Jimmy Hill into one of the toilet cubicles to discuss the crowd situation and requested that the kick-off was delayed in order to let the extraordinary turnout of fans from Bristol outside the ground to make their way through the turnstiles without putting anyone in danger. With the acceptance of myself and Coventry City manager Gordon Milne, it was agreed to delay the match by ten–twelve minutes. Due to the way the match concluded, I can see why people believe it was contrived, but I wish I had that foresight. At the time, I was purely focussed on the Bristol City-Coventry City game and the thought of having an advantage over Sunderland simply didn't cross my mind.

Understandably, there was a complaint from Sunderland, who were, quite naturally, upset at the conclusion of the match. The subsequent enquiry however, found nothing to substantiate the accusations and the result stood. For this reason, important league matches at the end of the season now kick off at the same time to avoid any team having an advantage. We will never know what might have happened that night if both games had kicked off at the same time. To say that the thought of the Everton-Sunderland game finishing early didn't cross anyone's minds at the time is debatable, but ultimately we will never know for sure. It is up to people to make their own minds up as to exactly what happened, or more importantly, the motives behind it. Alan says it wasn't planned and that is good enough for me. Ultimately we were safe and that was all that mattered to me.

The champagne flowed freely in the dressing room until we boarded the coach back to Ashton Gate. The drinks continued to flow as we made our way back south and Alan instructed all the players and staff to go straight to the boardroom on our arrival. As you'd expect, the mood in the boardroom was one of euphoric relief and Alan looked over at me amidst the chaos and gave me a wink to say well done. I was just pleased that I was able to help the club I had loved for so long. Had we been relegated, the £110,000 fee paid for me would have been lost revenue, along with the losses associated with not playing in the top-flight. I felt that in a small way, I had justified my return and repaid my debt to the fans.

After more champagne and celebration, we had a message to say that Platform One, a nightclub in the centre of Bristol, would stay open for us. It usually closed at 1.00am, but we all turned up at 3.00am to continue the private party. By 5.30am, people had started to disappear, exactly where, I don't know. I knew it had been a good night when I fell past the milkman who was whistling 'The Red, Red, Robin'. I was pissed out of my head and to this day I'm not sure exactly how I got home. Living in Nailsea, some nine miles away from the centre of Bristol, walking home certainly wasn't an option, so someone must have put me in a taxi which dropped me within walking distance from my home. I certainly wasn't the only one a bit worse for wear and we later found out that the directors had stayed in the boardroom until 6.00am. The whole city was buzzing and if you could have found a Rovers fan, I'm sure even they would have been pleased. After a busy season full of ups and downs, both personally and for the club, and a truly memorable night at the conclusion, it was difficult to see how it could be topped. Bleary-eyed and hung-over, I still woke up full of optimism on Friday morning, still high on the events of the night before. Going against my instinct, I looked to the future. It seemed bright, but my outlook was no doubt clouded by the alcohol and adrenalin in my system. Hindsight is the most wonderful thing, but nothing could have prepared me for the events, both personally and for Bristol City Football Club, that were about to unfold over the coming seasons. Football, by its often fragile and passionate nature, is precarious. Little did I know on that beautiful Friday morning that in the not-too-distant future, predicting what was around the corner would be seen as something no one in their right mind would attempt – at least not as far as football was concerned.

CHAPTER SIX

FROM MAGALUF TO HONG KONG

The hangover from the celebrations after the Coventry City match lasted days for players and supporters alike. Shortly after, Alan convinced the directors that the players deserved a week away and so the club arranged for all the staff to go on an end-of-season tour to Magaluf in Majorca. Well, to say it was a tour was stretching the truth somewhat, as the deal was that we would play one match against a local team. Despite it being completely free, some of the players didn't fancy a trip away. After a long season, some of the lads just wanted to get back with their families and go away on their own. I could understand that, of course, but this was only for one week and it was all paid for. Numbers became so important because we had to have at least twelve players for it to be considered an official club trip. In the end, we had to put kit-man Bill Tovey and physio Les Bardsley down as players for the trip to go ahead.

When we arrived at the resort, we realised immediately that a relaxing break might not be as easy to come by. By complete coincidence, Sunderland had decided to take their squad to the same place at the same time. Under normal circumstances, this wouldn't have been much of an issue. We would have had a bit of friendly banter and a good few drinks together. However, as a direct result of our 2–2 draw at Highfield Road on the final day of the season, Sunderland were the team relegated to Division Two. While we had gone there to celebrate, Sunderland were there to commiserate. The atmosphere on our arrival at the hotel was unbelievable. As soon as a few of the Sunderland boys realised who we were, shouts of 'cheating bastards' and jibes about the match being delayed deliberately became commonplace. In all honesty, if the boot had been on the other foot, I would have probably reacted in a similar way. Despite A.D.'s denial about any wrong-doing which, as I've mentioned, he stands by to this day – how on earth must it have looked to people on the outside? How did it look to the people of Sunderland? As Alan and Jimmy Hill had been good mates for such a long time, even I wasn't completely convinced, so I could understand their frustration both from a players' and supporters' perspective. Looking back, the policeman at Coventry did have a funny lop-sided walk and I wonder if it had anything to do with the brown envelope sticking out of his pocket. Never before had I seen a copper getting the beers in after a game! Just joking! But as you can tell by my own cynicism on the subject, I sympathised in some ways with the Sunderland lads.

After a few days in the sun, the comments did eventually turn into banter and a few of us would all meet up for a few drinks in the bar later in the evening. Frankly, my sympathy didn't last too long either and we carried on the celebrations where we had left off in Bristol. At the end of the day, we had done our job as players for Bristol City Football Club and that was that. Incidentally, while we were away, Sunderland lodged an appeal about the Bristol City–Coventry City fixture, but eventually it was thrown out. As promised, we played the game against the local team but it turned into a bit of a joke. Everyone got a game, including coaching staff Ken Wimshurst, Bill Tovey and Les Bardsley. After nearly two weeks of drinking, the game was never going to be anything more than a kick-about.

After returning from a subsequent break with Trish and the boys, I was eagerly looking forward to the new season. I always did and the mid-season period frequently seemed to drag. I was really up for the 1977–78 season and desperate to help ensure that the club did not end up in another relegation dog-fight. I had started training early and during pre-season felt in as good a shape as I had done at any point in my career. We opened the season at home to Wolves where we lost 3–2 in front of a tremendous crowd of over 25,000. Peter Cormack scored our goals but as well as putting up with a home defeat, I also picked up a neck injury after a collision with Wolves goalkeeper Phil Parkes. It was a fairly innocuous tumble, but I had strained the muscles in my neck. I missed the following four matches which included an away fixture at my old club Leicester City. I had also missed the corresponding fixture the previous season when I was out of the starting line-up and was an unused substitute. Alan allowed me to travel with the team, despite having to wear a specially-made collar, and I am pleased to say that the Leicester fans gave me a terrific reception. I even managed to have a quick cuppa with the tea lady and some of the ground staff after the game. I make no apologies for repeating myself when I say that everyone in Leicester has always been fantastic towards me. The lads earned a 0–0 draw at Filbert Street and we returned to Bristol where I continued to receive treatment from Les Bardsley. After a decent pre-season, I was frustrated at being out of the action and, after four league games, we were still looking for our first win having drawn two and lost two. The only bright spark in a disappointing August was a 1–0 victory over Stoke City in the League Cup where a rising young talent by the name of Kevin Mabbutt scored for us on his home debut at Ashton Gate.

I finally got the go-ahead to return to action on 10 September when we faced Norwich City at Carrow Road. After my strong performances at the end of the previous season, not only did the fans and management team have high expectations but I also set myself high standards to continue where I had left off. After a relatively quiet first twenty minutes, I turned to run back towards the half-way line. As I turned, I felt my knee collapse underneath me. I had never felt pain like it. I was carried off the pitch and taken into the dressing room where Les put an ice pack on it immediately. I knew it was serious, but everyone tried to reassure me that it might not be as bad as I had thought. It wouldn't happen today, but I made the long journey back across the width of England to Bristol on the coach with the rest of the lads. My knee was still heavily ice-packed, but it seemed to be doing little to stop the swelling or bruising. I had a scan on the Monday morning, but it showed very little. The second scan showed I had torn my cruciate ligaments and my cartilage, which would have to be removed. Thoughts were running through my mind at one-hundred miles an hour, particularly after watching what had happened to Paul Cheesley at first hand. I was admitted to St Mary's Hospital in Clifton in the centre of Bristol to have the operation. All I could think about was that this latest set-back could potentially be a career-ending injury, but I was determined that it wouldn't beat me. While I was in St Mary's, there were times when I really struggled to come to terms with what had happened. I lost a lot of weight and dropped down to around 10st 4lbs. When I eventually went home on the Saturday morning after the operation, I thought it would be the beginning of the recuperation period and the long road back to fitness. However, by mid-afternoon, I was back at St Mary's. As with Paul, the knee had blown up to three times its size with an infection. I spent a further ten days in hospital because of the infection and by this time I was getting really pissed off. There were a couple of occasions when things were so bad that I got a mate of mine, Brian Bronson, to give me a piggy back down the hill to the nearest pub just off of Park Street. I was gone for about an hour-and-a-half but the nurses – they were all nuns – had absolutely no idea – until the next morning that is. After a few pints, my pee-pot was nearly overflowing! 'Where have you been?' asked the Sister. 'You must have drunk a lot of water in the night!' Water, I thought, that's probably pure lager in there. I hate hospitals at the best of times, so the odd visit to the local made it a bit more bearable.

It may sound strange now, but I had major worries about my future in football as I lay in the hospital bed and later when I returned home. Today, key-hole surgery helps to reduce risk, infection and potentially time out of the game. In September 1977, I was staring at the end of my career. The months after the operation were tough. I knew they would be. Both Cheese (Paul Cheesley) and Les Bardsley had warned me that it would be a long time before the knee would be strong enough to do light exercise, let alone play a match in the top flight of English football. Frustration crept in and understandably, but not excusably, it had a knock-on effect on both my professional and private life. I would spend more time at the races, either as a punter or to accompany one of the various bookmakers or jockeys I had got to know, purely for a day out and to take my mind off of things. Apart from my family and friends, football had been my life since I could remember. There was a time I would have given anything to sit in the stand and watch Bristol City play. I would have given anything to watch my red-shirted heroes from a seat in the stand instead of through the railings or sneaking past the doorman. This, however, was different. I couldn't watch. I rarely went to an away fixture and I wasn't the most frequent visitor to Ashton Gate on a Saturday afternoon. My frustration was growing and watching Bristol City was now adding to the problem. The fact that the lads were struggling to hit any kind of consistent form, and I could do nothing to help to change matters, only made things worse.

With both Paul and me out of action for the foreseeable future, Alan Dicks dipped into the transfer market in November to secure the services of a much-needed striker. A.D.'s wheeler-dealings came up trumps again as he landed Manchester City's ex-England marksman

Joe Royle. In his first match against Middlesbrough, Joe gave the entire club the lift it needed. He scored all four goals in a 4–1 win at Ashton Gate, making him an instant hero on the terraces. He was also a very popular and likeable man in the dressing room and away from football, which helped endear him to players and staff alike. Unfortunately for both Joe and the team, after the Middlesbrough game, he would not score again for twelve matches. The next time he was on target was in February in a 3–0 win against the team I had injured my knee against five months earlier, Norwich City.

It was a bleak season for fans and players, having been knocked out of both cups by Third Division Wrexham and spending most of the season towards the foot of the table. Top-flight survival was guaranteed, however, and with thirty-five points in seventeenth place, both Bristol City and Chris Garland would be given another crack at making an impact on the First Division the following season – or so I hoped. Needless to say, I didn't make another appearance during the ill-fated 1977–78 season, but while my knee appeared to be a million miles away from full fitness, I did feel optimistic that a new season could bring new fortunes. In reality, my renewed optimism couldn't have been further from the truth. I played a few reserve games and even scored three goals in eight league and cup appearances during the 1978–79 season, but I knew things weren't right from the start. I don't care what anyone says, being injured back then was very different to a player being injured today. If you were injured, you weren't part of the squad and you were left out of everything. Whilst I was getting treatment in the morning and afternoon, the rest of the squad were training and preparing for big matches. It was really getting me down and I was desperate to get back to playing football and feeling a part of the club again. The 1979–80 season wasn't much better and my ten league appearances did little to help the team's plight. With Gary Collier becoming the first player to leave his club under the recently introduced Freedom of Contract and Norman Hunter joining Barnsley as player-coach, we were suddenly without our two central defenders. Not only were we still struggling to score goals, but we now had trouble keeping them out of our net. You didn't need a manual or a so-called expert to tell you this was a recipe for disaster. With little money to spend and key members of the squad missing or departed, we were relegated after four seasons in Division One. The pain and despair of watching the club I had loved since being a small boy fall into Division Two was unbearable. Not just because I was a supporter, but because, as an injured player, I was almost powerless to intervene. Realistically, I also knew that my chance of playing again in the top-flight of English football was gone.

On the plus side, the only good thing to come out of that season was the birth of our daughter Jessica. Jess was born in the BRI in Bristol late in the evening of 15 November. It was, of course, a very special moment. I loved the boys, but we had always wanted a girl. As with Adam and Ryan, I was there for the birth – a hat trick (!) – which went smoothly, with the staff at the hospital doing a wonderful job. I celebrated in typical 'I've just become a father again' style by wetting the baby's head a few times. Of course, I had no way of knowing that years later she would travel the world and represent England at netball.

The start of the new season saw no real improvement. I was sub for three of the first four games, which were all drawn and actually started a match in the home game with Swansea, which we lost one-nil. It was around then that Alan Dicks was dismissed and Bob Houghton, the former Malmo manager, took over. I was still having problems with my knee and didn't get a look in until October–November time, when I played in four games on the trot. I managed to score in the last of those, against Blackburn, but then got a bollocking for not marking their centre half when he joined the attack. I think Houghton was looking for an excuse for not playing me. I played a few more times – my last match was a cup game at Derby in the January – but I was still having problems with my knee and ligaments. Houghton had a lot of contacts in Sweden and fixed it up to send me out there to get match fit and to build up my confidence. I went on a six month's loan with Vasteras AFK in the Swedish Second Division, having travelled up to London with the club secretary to negotiate terms. Everything went OK with the negotiations. The club were providing a fully furnished two-bedroomed apartment, a car and £300 a week – £75 a week more than my most recent contract at City. This would turn out to be my biggest salary in football – 'big time Charlie' – ten years after leaving City on £50 a week for £60 a week at Chelsea, then Leicester – £125 a week – and back to City on £125. Later, when I had a new contract at City, I got £225 a week, the most I ever earned at the club. When I told Joe Royle about the new deal he said, 'well done, I'm paying that in tax each week!' 'Dicksie' had done me again. Money matters were never my forte, as you'll probably conclude by the end of this book. I had even paid my own removal expenses to go back to City.

But back to Sweden. It was April and the season had only just started after a hard winter. I had flown into Stockholm and then onto Vasteras to be met by the club's chairman. Then to a hotel in town, where the press and television people were waiting for interviews. The club manager and captain were also there and we went off after talking to the media, to discuss the season ahead. There was another club in Vasteras – IFK Vasteras – and the clubs were great rivals (bit like City and Rovers in Bristol). The chairman showed me an article in the local paper by their manager, former Wolves coach Sammy Chung, saying AFK had made a big mistake by signing me, that I had a dodgy knee and wasn't the player I used to be. Thanks Sam, I love you too. But, as they say, he who laughs last... We played his team in our third game, with a crowd of over nine thousand there for the derby. It was a cracking game, with Sammy's team two up at the break. Our coach changed the shape to a 4-4-2 formation at half time, with me playing a free role between midfield and the strikers. Within minutes of the second half we had pulled a goal back, only to concede a silly goal twenty minutes from time. Obviously Sammy considered me a non-threat and I was suddenly finding myself with plenty of space in and around the eighteen-yard box. I had set up the lad from Finland to score, then flicked on a corner for him to score again. Then it was my turn to celebrate, as I volleyed in the equaliser. We were pleased, with only minutes to go, to have saved something from the game, but then we were awarded a free kick on the right side of the box. There were lots of shouting and dummy runs, but a well-rehearsed routine saw the ball finish up in the net. Our supporters went crazy and, as the ref blew for time, rushed onto the pitch. A great result and I was being carried off the pitch by the supporters in only my third game.

Sammy Chung kept very low key for the rest of the season!

I was still taking things carefully at training, restricting myself to working with weights and cross-country runs. As the season progressed we were doing OK and kept our promotion hopes up. The lads out there were great to me and there was always a group of us that went for a drink after games, although it was expensive – you never went to the bar and shouted 'who wants a drink?' Of course the summers were lovely and Trish and the kids flew over to join me for a month. Sweden is a beautiful country and very clean. We would spend days on the small islands surrounded by lakes – a great way of life.

As the season progressed we kept in touch at the top of the table. By now I had become quite popular with AFK's fanatical supporters and most nights they would gather outside my apartment and sing songs. After the struggle I'd had with my knee injury over the past three seasons, it felt good to be appreciated. I will never forget Bob Houghton's last words to me before I went to Sweden – ' Do well over there and there will be a new contract waiting for you.' As I had been receiving rave reports both in the local and the Stockholm press, I found it very disappointing to be totally ignored when I drove fifty miles to watch City in a pre-season game. He didn't give me five minutes to check out how I was playing. It was obvious that, no matter how well I played, he had no intention of offering me a new deal. I must admit, it knocked me back, as I still had two months on my contract and nothing to play for, except to do my best to help Vasteras get promotion to the top Swedish division. Although I wasn't scoring many goals, my contribution and overall play was probably the best it had been since my injury problems. I did get the chance to catch up with a few old friends when Chelsea came out to play a friendly with IFK. I went over to watch them train and caught up with a few old mates like Mickey Droy, Ray Wilkins, Ian Britton and a few others. They asked me how good IFK were and who were their best players. I told them there shouldn't be a problem. How wrong could I be? Chelsea were far too casual and got hammered five-nil – a result that saved 'my friend' Sammy Chung from getting the sack.

With time passing quickly and Trish and the children having gone back to England, we only had five weeks left to get promotion. The chairman wanted me back the following season, even if they didn't go up. The last five games were crucial and it went right to the wire – the last game, at home, against a mid-table side. It was a promotion disaster in front of 10,000 hopeful supporters. We couldn't cope with the unusually wet and windy conditions, got well and truly beaten 4-1 and missed promotion by just one point. Amazingly, though, the group of supporters who had been following and supporting me all over Sweden, ran onto the pitch at the end, lifted me onto their shoulders and carried me back to the dressing room, as a thank-you for my efforts during the season. The chairman invited everybody back to his house for a drink and, to my surprise, presented me with a club shirt signed by all the players and a big card signed by everyone at the club. It was a fitting end to my six months at Vasteras. As for Sammy Chung, he didn't turn up to the airport to wave me off!

On the plane going back to England I had time to reflect on my time in Sweden, where the season is shorter because of the severe weather. I played in thirteen of the sixteen league games, scoring four goals. But that statistic doesn't tell the whole story, as my 'assists' were by far the highest at the club. The reason I missed those three games was because I had stepped on a broken bottle while walking in one of the lakes and had to have six stitches. I definitely knew that I had obtained a great level of fitness and proved to myself that I could play at a decent standard. Now it was time to see Bob Houghton on the Monday and we all knew what he was going to say. He didn't disappoint me and offered me a free transfer there and then, making it obvious there was no chance of a new contract, or of playing for Bristol City again. Well, he was proved to be wrong on that one.

Having missed the start of the 1981/82 season and been told I wasn't part of Houghton's plans I asked to go on the transfer list. Basically, I was just playing out what remained of my contract. Houghton didn't want me, he just didn't fancy me in his team. Some people say his head was on the block and that he was under pressure. Well, if you can call living in The Dragonara, drinking champagne and smoking cigars with the directors pressure – yes, that's pressure! I did get a game for City towards the end of November, against Burnley at home. I scored, but we lost 3-2 and Bob Houghton again blamed me for not marking one of the Burnley lads when they got one of their goals. I didn't feature again until making a substitute appearance against Huddersfield in January. By the time we got a home draw with Villa in the Cup, Bob Houghton was gone and his assistant, Roy Hodgson was in the chair. He didn't last long though. We played really well against Villa that night and were a bit unlucky to lose one-nil. After the game we were told that eight of us – myself, Gerry Sweeney, Julian Marshall, Peter Aitken, David Rodgers, Jimmy Mann, Geoff Merrick and Trevor Tainton – were to report at the ground the next morning. That was unusual, to be called in the morning after a game. We knew that the club was in trouble, but we didn't really know what was in store. Tear up your contracts or the club will go bankrupt and fold, that was the ultimatum. They wanted to get rid of us – in the twilight of our careers in some cases – but there were other big earners who weren't considered because the club knew that they could sell them. I was on good money – £260 a week – but it's not good money if you're suddenly asked to accept ten pence in the pound. I was owed money from my last transfer, with it being spread over my wages – I think I lost about £3,750 – a lot of money in those days. If those directors had managed their businesses like they managed Bristol City, they'd have gone bankrupt. They had wasted thousands, but made us the scapegoats. We had just over a week to make a decision. The PFA were called in, but, quite frankly, they weren't much good. Three or four of the lads were in the side that played at Newport County in what could have been City's last-ever game. Quite ironic when you think that I live in Newport these days. I wasn't playing, but went to the game. It was such a weird and horrible situation. We had until midday on the Wednesday after the Newport game to give our answer. It went right to the wire and we finally agreed about half an hour before the deadline and the club was saved.

Andy Llewellyn summed it up when he said that if it wasn't for the Ashton Gate Eight there wouldn't be a Bristol City and players like him would never have got their chance. We did get a testimonial game and I'm grateful to the 6,000 who turned up for it, but when you divide the gate receipts by eight, it doesn't amount to much. After that we all went together to sign on the dole. Some of the lads got fixed up with short-term contracts elsewhere, but Geoff (Merrick) and I managed to get fixed up with a team in Hong Kong and went as soon as we could, getting away from all the fuss and palaver in Bristol. We had six-month contracts and there were a few top players like Bobby Moore and Alan Ball out there. Tommy Hutchinson, who is a football development coach at City, and Phil Boyer were also there. If you were with a good club you were treated fine. The rest of the teams were there just to make up the numbers. Our manager was Portuguese and the story goes that he got the job by mistake, a case of mistaken identity at the airport. The coach was Chinese and, at over seventeen stone, didn't inspire confidence. It was easy enough to keep fit though, as with the heat the pounds just dropped off you. The fact that we were in a non-air-conditioned flat didn't make life any easier. And when you were out in a restaurant it was nothing to see rats under your table while you were eating. We used to play at the only ground there,

Happy Valley. We'd train at six-thirty in the morning because of the heat. Often we'd go straight to training from one of the night clubs where all the ex-pats would meet up. Hong Kong is a dangerous place on your own. Before a game they'd often carry a pig around the penalty area for good luck. It didn't do us any good – we lost our first match 4-0. The main problem with the game out there though was the corruption, especially in football. There are so many betting syndicates that it wasn't unusual to find players on both sides had taken money to lose. Not the English players – they certainly never approached me – but I'm sure some of the locals. Geoff didn't believe it was bent to start with, but I think he did eventually. A lot of money was won and lost on their football matches, although we were often chasing the owners for our wages. At the end of our contracts, when we made sure we'd been paid, we booked our flights and left a note – 'Thank you very much – bye.' Having said that, it was a great experience and Geoff even considered going back for a second time.

When I got home Joe Royle called to say he was coming to Bristol for an interview for the City job, Hodgson having left not long after Houghton. I told him not to bother – it was common knowledge that the job was going to Terry Cooper. And it was Terry who persuaded me to come back to Bristol City for a third and final time.

CHAPTER SEVEN

ASHTON GATE TO CIVVY STREET

By the time I'd got back from Hong Kong there was a completely new set-up at Bristol City, with – as I had foretold my friend Joe Royle – Terry Cooper in the manager's chair. The new company – Bristol City (1982) Ltd – had a new board, chaired by Leslie Kew, alongside Deryn Coller, Chris Curling, Ken Sage and Ivor Williams. And, although this new group were determined to stamp out all the extravagancies and bad money-management that had nearly seen the club fold, they recognised that my ten years service to the club merited a testimonial and let me have use of the ground free. A fund-raising committee was set up, including Reg Bell the bookmaker (who I was later to work for), Roger Smith and Bill Taylor, who managed the local casino. There was to be a sporting dinner, golf day and a match at Ashton Gate, the new City team against an all-star eleven. A lot of my old team mates played in the all-stars, with Geoff Merrick, Gerry Sweeney and Gowie (Gerry Gow) in the line-up. Paul Cheesley also turned out and – the icing on the cake – George Best. I'd always been good friends with George over the years. We would bump into each other at sporting dinners and so on. He used to spend a lot of time in London during his playing days and you would see him down the King's Road or Alexander's Restaurant. He would always stop for a chat and ask how you were getting on. We went through George's agent – Bill McMurdo – to get him. Obviously George would be paid for coming down and we set up personal appearances with various businesses to help meet the fee his agent had asked for. He arrived in Bristol in style in a golden Rolls Royce and the local media were keen to pursue his romantic interest with actress and former Miss World, Mary Stavin (it always was the simple pleasures in life for George!). Mind you, the media were always interested in whatever George was doing and George, being George, never disappointed them. Lots of people thought he wouldn't turn up, but Bestie was very good and didn't let me down. Around three-and-a-half thousand came to the game and apart from raising a few thousand quid, it also opened the door for a final spell with City. My two boys were the mascots, and I was really proud having them run out with me for the game.

George was brilliant, he still had it, he really turned it on. Even then, at the age of thirty-six, it was obvious that he should still have been playing professionally. Terry's young City side won 4–3, although George scored a trademark goal for us. I think he was taking the Mick a bit, beating two players in typical 'Bestie' style, before sliding the ball through the keeper's legs. I got the other two goals – a header and a volley. I wasn't really fit and hadn't played for months, but my first thoughts were that I'd gone out on a high. The last thing I expected, as we all headed for the local casino for a bit of a bash afterwards, was for Terry to ask me to consider coming back to City. He'd played in the testimonial – scored a cracking goal actually – and obviously considered I could still do a job for the team, as well as helping some of the younger players. Short of experienced strikers, Terry asked if I would play for the club on a week-to-week basis as a non-contract player. A businessman put up my £100 a week 'expenses' and so, four months after my testimonial game and about a year since my last first-team game and the Ashton Gate Eight saga, I was running out for City once again.

One or two of the lads couldn't understand how I could go back, but Bristol City's been my team since I was five and it was a chance to put the red shirt back on – my swan song. I always say it was the people who ran the club who were to blame for the disaster of 1982, not Bristol City the team.

It felt good to put on a City shirt again and run out through the tunnel and, after all the Ashton Gate Eight business, I received a warm welcome from the crowd. On New Year's Day we played Swindon at home. Unfortunately I received a bad cut over my right eye when colliding with the goalkeeper. We managed to scrape a draw, but the next morning I woke up to find both eyes completely closed and as black as the ace of spades. My wife drove me to the ground, as it was dangerous for me to drive. I was just walking into the treatment room where TC (Terry Cooper) was checking on injuries before the following day's game at Darlington. He said, 'see you in the morning, you'll be alright, just stand up front and be a nuisance.' My own feeling was that there was no way I could play if it did not improve overnight and, if anything, the swelling was far greater in the morning. But off I went, to score what was to be my last goal for Bristol City.

Darlington FC's old ground – Feethams. What a dump! I had gone full circle from Bristol City in the old Third Division when I joined as an apprentice, to the top level, playing at Stamford Bridge, Old Trafford and Wembley and now all the way back down again. Darlington on a wet Monday night. One small bath, no showers and one light hanging down from the ceiling, the wires close to the bath. The place was falling to bits. Then, to top it all, the game was delayed because a dead pigeon was tangled up in one of the goal nets. The game was terrible, but I did manage that last goal to save us a point. And at the end of it all, TC says well done, you've got ten minutes to get dressed as the chip shop shuts early on Bank Holidays. That's how tight money was at the club then. Up to Darlington and back same day and fish-and-chips on the coach home – it can be a glamorous life being a footballer! I managed four more games after that.

I'd been playing for City on a week-by-week basis and been grateful for one last chance to run out for my team again and help them through a difficult period. Terry Cooper was doing a good job trying to turn around the club's fortunes after the disasters of the previous few years. He was a nice fella and proved to be a good manager. After all, he went on to get City promotion and anyone who could do that – given their immediate past problems of that time – has to be a good manager. I mean, he started off by having to play most of the youth team. Of course it had to come to an end, I knew that and, after what was to be my last game – Scunthorpe away in early February – TC thanked me for all I'd done to help the club out. Now that they had got through the initial crisis it was the end of my Bristol City career. Now I had to find a job. But what?

A friend of mine had his own fruit-and-veg round and I thought well, in my neck of the woods there's Clevedon, Portishead and Nailsea, I could do that. I could set up a round and make a living out of that, without living off 'the Social.' And that's what I did. I did that for about two years. I managed to establish a number of regular customers in the area, including four or five old people's homes – good orders at £30 or £40 a time, which in those days was a lot of money. It helped that I was an ex-footballer and I'd often be engaged in conversation with customers who wanted to talk about soccer and my experiences in the game. All very flattering and nice to be asked. Still, it was a living. The trouble was when I finished on a Friday I'd be down the pub – The Farmhouse at Nailsea was one of my watering holes – for a few bevvies. If I wasn't gambling the money away, I was boozing it away. OK, I know it's the working man's prerogative to have a beer now and again at the end of a day's work, but I wasn't doing myself any favours. On top of that, I was beginning to have enough of getting up at four in the morning and that's every day, not once or twice a week. It wears you down in the end.

It was during that time that I got a call from my old mate Gerry Gow, who had taken over as manager of Yeovil Town, asking if I could help out on the coaching side. I'd made a complete break from football – apart from turning out for a couple of games with Gloucester City to help out some friends there – but I'd always wanted to get involved in coaching, although my initial thoughts were to help coach youngsters. But there was no youth set-up at Yeovil, who were a non-league side in those days. 'Gowie' wanted my assistance to help steer the first team away from relegation. So, I used to drive down in my van on a Tuesday and Thursday night and take the coaching. He was on a hiding to nothing there, but they used to get good gates, around 1,300 for home games, even if they were bottom of the league. They were struggling at the wrong end of the table and we had to get them out of trouble. The chairman there was Gerry Lock – a good bloke who, sadly, later died in a car crash. The team needed strengthening and I managed to persuade my friend Ian Botham to play. I used to watch him playing cricket for Somerset and we would usually have a few beers after a game. Ian's always good company – good for a laugh and a joke. The conversation would inevitably turn to soccer. We all know what a great cricketer he was, but he could also play football – he'd played for Scunthorpe and you don't play League soccer without having some ability as a footballer. Of course, Ian is from the Yeovil area and the idea of playing for Yeovil Town definitely appealed to him. I think we got between 3,000 and 4,000 for his first game. OK, he was a crowd puller, he was the famous 'larger than life' cricket celebrity Ian Botham. But, make no mistake, he could play football. He did well for us – there were others at the club not as good as him in the team. Yes, he had a different lifestyle to us, but he'd never let anyone down, either through his ability on the pitch or his commitment to help. He played his last game for us just twelve hours before flying off for a cricket tour of the West Indies.

I enjoyed being involved in football again, even down to strapping up Ian's dodgy ankle before games. 'Gowie' was hoping to progress onwards and upwards and ultimately get the club into the Football League. His priority then was to avoid relegation. I know he was looking to make his mark during his time there, and, if you remember his fearsome tackling, you'll know what I mean when I say he certainly left his mark on the legs of one or two opponents! I wouldn't mind betting that there are more than a few former Southern League players who still carry the scars from their encounters with him to this day! Mind you, one of his own team mates – Ian Botham no less – nearly left a mark on him when Gowie decided to substitute him. If looks could have killed when Ian walked off that pitch... On the other side of the coin, when I tried to substitute Gerry during one game, he didn't take it too well. 'You can't sub me – I'm the boss!' was his astonished reaction to being called off.

Sometimes, though, it was best to get him off the pitch before he got sent off. Another ex-City lad on the books there was Tom Ritchie, who had a player/coach role. A good lad Tom – worked on the post. Perhaps I should have gone down that road when you consider the number of ex-City lads that became posties – Louie (Andy Llewellyn), Gerry Sweeney, Gibbo (Mike Gibson).... We could have had a good team!

I did the coaching at Yeovil for about a season. The trouble was, by the time I got home from there on Tuesdays and Thursdays and got to bed, it was time to get up again for my fruit-and-veg business. Well, you can't go on like that, you'll end up killing yourself and the money from Yeovil – I was getting about £20 a week – was just about covering my petrol. On top of that, business wasn't so good. In the end I was giving the veg away. You'd deliver to some of the older customers and they'd want two potatoes, three sprouts, an apple and an orange. You'd say 'that's thirty-six pence please... oh forget it, don't worry, have it on me.' Things continued to get worse. What little I was earning was going straight to the bookies and the bills weren't getting paid. It was very depressing. At one time I felt I had the world at my feet and now I was in the pits of despair. It got so bad that I seriously considered ending it all. In fact, it went beyond just considering it. I drove out to Nailsea moors one night with a bottle of tablets. I sat there thinking about the way my life had turned out and how it all seemed so hopeless. I sat there for ages, feeling more and more sorry for myself and wondering if I'd have the guts to take that final step and swallow the contents of the bottle. I don't really know how long I was there, but a local farmer – Danny Baker – had spotted my van and came across to see what was going on. I'd known Danny and his family for years, particularly his sons, who were – still are I think – involved in the local football scene. He sussed what was happening straight away. 'Come on Chris – this isn't doing any good. Let's go inside and talk about it.' And he took me back to his place and sat chatting to me and talking it out of my system over a couple of cups of tea. I still don't know what would have happened if he hadn't shown up. What I did come to realise is that what I was considering was selfish and a coward's way out. Obviously I feel for anyone that's been so low that they even contemplate suicide, but it's not the answer. You have to think of the pain you're going to cause to those who love you and the mess you're leaving for them to clear up.

To say I was in desperate need of a change is an understatement, but something different did come along that offered a new challenge and fresh hope. John Lillington, who'd been club secretary at City, had a haulage company. Part of that included wine distribution and he asked whether I'd like to take over that side of the business. I thought to myself, 'I could make a go of that.' I was quite interested in wine and, not surprisingly, had quite a few contacts in the pubs, restaurants and wine bars – most of them knew me from my playing days. It was quite ironic that now I'd be delivering to places that I'd previously been drinking in until three or four o'clock in the morning. Now I would be taking my wine into them, instead of leaving with a bellyfull of their wine inside me! It was going OK to start with. My friends in the racing game – bookmakers, jockeys and so on – were good customers and would often order crates of the stuff. And, with a garage full of stock, I was never short of a bottle of wine. But then came the problems. Around Christmas time I faced stiff opposition with the major off licences. I remember, I think it was Julian Flooks, offering their customers credit – 'have your wine in December, as much drink as you want and you don't have to pay until the end of January.' That was bad enough, but, on top of that, they were offering discounts. Well, I couldn't compete with that – no small business could. Just to keep up with the competition, I began letting some of my customers have credit (I think one or two had dodgy credit ratings) to help them out so that I didn't lose their custom. You could sense it was going to go wrong – that something bad was going to happen. And it did.

Come the end of January, start of February, when I went to pick my money up, some of them had closed down. Some of them owed me £200 or more and you just can't afford to lose that sort of money when you're a small business. You end up ordering more stock, to try and sell more to recoup your losses. It becomes a vicious circle. Those sort of situations aren't a real problem for the big suppliers, who can afford the odd bad debt. But for someone like me, operating on a much smaller scale, it was a disaster. You need the cash up-front in order to keep the business going. The end was inevitable and I was declared bankrupt. It was an awful time. We had to downsize and sell the house. We didn't have any choice. We moved out of the beautiful old farmhouse that we'd bought when I came back to Bristol and moved down the road to another property, a detached house just behind The White Lion, another of my old haunts. To make matters worse, I was still having the odd flutter – and losing.

There's an old saying – if you can't beat 'em, join 'em. Reg Bell, the bookmaker who'd helped me set up my testimonial, along with another bookie called Gerry Parker, contacted me and asked if I was any good at maths. I said I wasn't too bad, it was one of my better subjects at school and I could certainly work out a few bets. After all, I used to go racing whenever I could – I loved racing, going to local tracks like Bath and Chepstow. Anyway, they offered me a job as a bookie's clerk. Three or four days a week I was away with the bookmaking – earning around £30 a day and losing £40! With hindsight, it wasn't the best career move I ever made. Ever since I was a youngster I'd enjoyed racing, so it was easy to get sucked in. I'd made good friends with a number of jockeys – John Francombe, Steve Knight, Kevin Mooney, who rode for The Queen Mother. They became very good pals. I used to play in the injured jockey's charity matches to raise money for them, which they appreciated and they returned the favour later when I had my health problems. What goes around comes around. There's only one sure thing with gambling. You might get lucky now and then, but it doesn't matter what or who you know, you'll get sucked in and the bookie wins in the end. I used to get some good tips from my contacts, but still ended up losing. Ok, you get the odd good day – I think the best I did at a day's racing was winning five grand. But the bookie will get that back off you many times over, believe me.

There was one time when Steve Knight was riding for Andy Turner, a very good trainer. He gave me a ring and asked if I could pick him up and take him to Newbury Races. No problem. I picked him up and on the way in we were discussing his big race, a novice hurdle. I said his ride stood a good chance and he said yes, but they reckon Mary Rimmel's horse is a certainty. I looked at the betting in the *Sporting Life* and Mary's horse was eight or nine to one and Steve's was at five to two. I said if this was a flat race your horse would win easily. Steve said, 'he jumps brilliantly at home, no problem, but this horse of Mary's, everyone's talking about it and saying it was going to be a champion hurdler'. When we got to the track, I looked at the betting and Steve's horse had gone out to about ten to one, and Mary's horse was odds-on favourite, something like six to four on. I thought the favourite's bound to win. With odds like that you would, wouldn't you? It looked like a certainty and Steve's comments about how good it was clinched it. I backed it. Five minutes later the race starts. Two fences from home Steve's about fifteen lengths clear – he absolutely romped home at about twelve or fourteen to one. I was being sick behind the stand. As he walked towards the jockey's room after the race he asked 'Did you have a bet ?' 'Yes – I had a bet alright, I backed the favourite.' 'Idiot,' he replied. So much for insider knowledge.

I'd had the one season at Yeovil and was wondering what was next when I got the chance to manage Minehead in the Premier Division of the Western League. They were struggling and the chairman, Nolan Elston, told me that they couldn't afford to be relegated. 'If we go down it'll be a disaster,' were his words. I brought in a few lads from Yeovil and we did OK. Nolan Elston was totally committed to the club. He was paying the wages out of his own pocket, it wasn't costing the club a penny. In those days the lads were getting £30 or £40 a week, good money for Western League football. We did what we set out to do and kept the club in the Premier Division.

It was while I was at Minehead that a new career opportunity came up – insurance. There was a chap from the Midlands, Birmingham I think, who was a Minehead supporter. He used to stop and have a drink after the game. He had moved down to Minehead and was an agent for Royal Life Insurance. We were having a drink after one game and he said, 'you ought to go into insurance, you'd do really well.' I wasn't keen, but he said 'come on, give it a go and see how you get on.' I filled in all the paperwork and went up to Liverpool for two weeks for a course. I got to the hotel and the first thing I learnt was don't take your eye off your suitcase when you're checking in. There was a girl standing behind me waiting to check in and by the time she turned around her bag was gone, somebody had had it away and calmly walked out the door. She was on the same course as me. I felt so sorry for her. That could have been my case. You know what it's like when you check into a hotel. You go to reception, put your case down and check in. That was all the time it took for the thief to pick hers up and stroll out into the street and away.

I later found out that this scam had been going on at that particular hotel for ages and that it was not unusual for people to end up leaving after their stay with less luggage than they'd arrived with.

It was while I was taking the course that I bumped into Graham Day, who'd played for Rovers for years. He was also taking an insurance course. So I told my manager and he signed Graham on as well. Graham's a good bloke and it was nice to have a friendly face around with the same sense of humour, the footballing background and so on. I got through the course successfully and was given my patch – Bristol down to Cornwall – selling insurance, pensions and investments.

I had been with Royal Life for about eighteen months or so when I bumped into Jim Evans, who used to be the commercial manager at City. He was working for the Frazer Group, independent financial advisers who had their HQ in Leicester. Having spent an enjoyable part of my career in Leicester, I thought that was a good omen when he offered me a position with his company. In fact, he offered jobs to both me and Graham. My round would be much bigger – Bristol to Blackpool – but, with a new car and an increase in salary, it seemed too good to be true. Two years later it proved to be just that. But, at the time, it seemed a good move, although some of the company's marketing strategy was a bit off. I remember they had this idea of selling insurance to long-distance lorry drivers. They sent me up to Motherwell for a week to try and drum up some business from the drivers when they drove in at the end of their shifts. I was to team up with another chap from the company who I'd not met before and between us we were to try and make some sales. Anyway, we met at the hotel we'd been booked into. I noticed he walked with a bit of a limp, but didn't think any more of it. We were sharing a room with two single beds – a bit like when you're away with the football team.

We'd checked in and got to our room and I was in the bathroom having a wash and cleaning my teeth, that sort of thing, when I looked into the bathroom mirror and saw him on the bed.

I had to look twice – he was unscrewing his wooden leg. Talk about a shock. I wondered why he'd been walking awkwardly, but had no idea. Don't get me wrong. I'm the last person to take the Mick out of somebody with a medical affliction, but to see someone you've not met before and who you've got to work alongside, unscrewing his leg, it does come as a bit of a shock. Anyway, we set off to the lorry depot to meet the drivers as they came in. This would be about four in the morning and these blokes had just finished an eight-or-nine hour shift. Trying to sell anything to anyone in those circumstances is not a good idea. You'd say, 'excuse me sir, would you be interested in buying a pension plan?' You can imagine the sort of response we got. They were knackered and all they wanted to do was to get home, see the missus, have a bite to eat and get some kip. We had a week of that – a complete waste of time, probably dreamt up by some brain-dead whizz kid. I don't think we made a single sale. Another of their daft schemes was to have a stand at the annual TUC meeting in Blackpool. I was up there with Graham for the week, but, as an idea, it was dead in the water. People attending weren't interested in buying pensions and so on, that wasn't why they were there. As ideas go, it was right up there with the lorry drivers' promotion, a complete waste of time and money.

On the plus side, one of the good things about being with a Leicester-based company was that I could catch up with a few old team mates from my days at Filbert Street. Sometimes I'd have to go up for a meeting or whatever and I'd find time for a chat with Jon Sammels, or Alan Birchenall or the late Keith Weller – what a player he was. About one month in three I used to have to stop over, so I had more of a catch-up with them. Not surprisingly, I never got to meet up with Jeff Blockley, who I'd had the training-ground bust-up with, although I have bumped into him at PFA dos and he always came up to me to say hello and shake my hand. I'm not sure that his wife ever forgave me for that incident, though.

It was while I was with the Frazer Group that I began to have serious concerns about my health. There were little things I became aware of, like starting to shuffle a bit when I walked. Occasionally my speech wasn't quite right, a bit slurred. My hands would shake.

I'm sure there were plenty of people who thought I'd been out on the booze. My kids thought it was funny at first and I'd pretend, even try to kid myself, that it was the result of years of taking knocks playing football. Probably nothing to worry about, but in the end I decided to get expert advice. I made an appointment at the Bristol Royal Infirmary for a check up. They did their tests and told me straight away. The doctor said: 'you do know that you've got Parkinson's?'

CHAPTER EIGHT

TO HELL AND BACK

Parkinson's Disease? It's one of those medical condition phrases, like MS and cancer, that fills you full of dread. I knew it was serious, but still didn't quite know what it all meant. The specialist spelt it out. He explained that it's a disease that progressively attacks the nervous system. He pointed out that the shakes would get worse, that the left or right side of my body would be affected, silly things like my handwriting would be not so good and that I would be on drugs for the rest of my life. To say I was in a daze would be an understatement. But, he added that it was treatable, although, at the worst, I could end up in a wheelchair in five years. Well that was nearly twenty years ago and I proved that wrong. They put me on specialist drugs straight away – Simemet – six a day. That was to increase the dopamine, a chemical produced by brain cells. With Parkinson's, there is a progressive loss of brain cells, which means that less dopamine is produced and transported to the area of the brain that co-ordinates body movement. There were other anti-Parkinsonism drugs that I had to take, up to thirty a day at one time, and I think I was used as a sort of guinea pig to start with.

I decided to keep my condition a secret from everyone. Well, not quite everyone. I had a chat about it with my manager; after all, I did need to take some time off now and again for hospital appointments and so on. He was very good about it, even joked that they wouldn't be making me redundant – although, ironically, I was made redundant in the end, but that was something separate from my illness. But I didn't tell my family, not even Trish. And my Dad was very ill at the time and Mum had enough on her plate without me coming out with a bombshell like that. I kept it quiet, praying perhaps they'd come up with a cure. I would go off to work as normal and just have an hour off when I had to see the specialist. I went eighteen months keeping it to myself. To top it all, about three months after I had been diagnosed and was trying to cope with that, we were called to a meeting at head office. We were told that the Frazer Group was in trouble and that there would be redundancies. It was a case of 'last in, first out' – and that was me. But it was only a matter of time before the rest would have to go. Graham stayed a little longer, but the writing was on the wall. Out of work and struggling with Parkinson's – this was not a good time. Trish was working part-time at a local furnishings shop in Nailsea and I was on disability living allowance – knowing that there was no chance of getting another job. Eventually I had to tell her and the kids. It was getting harder to hide my illness from them – it wasn't getting better, it was getting worse – the shakes and so on, and I was becoming more introvert. It was coming up to Christmas and I knew I had to tell them. Don't ask me why I chose then. It certainly wasn't the best of times to break something like that – a bit naughty given the time of year – but there probably wasn't a good time. When I did tell them it was a relief, it was out in the open. They obviously knew that there was something wrong and I was glad to get it off my chest. I should have told them earlier, but your emotions are all over the place in those circumstances. You're trying to shield them, protect them from the knowledge, the fear that you're carrying with you every day. It was bad enough coping with the financial crash at Bristol City and then everything else going wrong on the work front, culminating in the redundancy from Frazers. That was depressing enough for them without throwing Parkinson's into the equation.

By this time I'd stopped going to sporting dinners, football matches and so on. I didn't want people to see the way I was. I was also having problems with some of the drugs.

You know what it's like when you go to the doctor's. Whatever the doctor says you do. He prescribes something for your problem and you take it. In my case, one particular drug I'd been prescribed was Mirapexin. This is supposed to help control the body's involuntary movements, but it has side effects, like causing obsession, which, for a gambler like me, is all you need! It can also cause drowsiness and you can suddenly nod off, whether you're out, with company or even driving. That's happened to me a few times and if I'd been on my own behind the wheel I'd be dead by now. It's a dangerous drug and I've heard that it's since become the subject of massive law suits in Canada.

I think a few people had suspected that there was something seriously wrong with my health and it became public knowledge after

I got a call from Roger Malone, who used to cover local soccer for HTV. Somehow he'd got wind that there was something seriously wrong – I don't know how – and got in touch and asked for an interview. The funny thing was, after we'd finished the interview, he took me out for a pub lunch on expenses and bought champagne. What the hell was I supposed to be celebrating?! It was front page news in the local press and soon in the national press, which I found a bit strange, as there are people in far worse conditions than me. I suppose it's because I was in the public eye as an ex-footballer who had gone through all the Ashton Gate Eight hassle and all that stuff. Once it was in the public arena I received calls from old team mates – people like Geoff Merrick, Paul Cheesley and Gerry Sweeney from 'the City,' plus lads from Chelsea and Leicester – Alan Birchenall, Tommy Baldwin, Alan Hudson, 'Ossie,' Ronnie Harris, Ian Hutchinson. They were very good, very supportive. They would ring up and be encouraging and ask what they could do to help. I also got a call from Joe (Royle) who said, 'I'll have a word with Fergie (Alex Ferguson) and get Man United down for you.' And he was as good as his word. Fergie said he'd bring his team down for a fund raiser, but they were fully booked for a year and it would have to be twelve months down the line. And sure enough, he didn't let me down, although it did cause a problem later. Nolan Elston at Minehead was another to give me a call, offering to help. We set up two successive weekends involving a dinner, golf day and some matches. He'd contacted Alan Ball, who was at Exeter at the time and he promised to bring a team along, Joe would bring his Oldham side and also there was to be a Minehead versus an all-stars team. It went well. The fund was launched at a sporting evening at the club on the Friday, with Ossie (Peter Osgood) and Frank Worthington the guest speakers – what a couple of characters! Soccer doesn't seem to have characters like that any more. Sadly, Ossie's no longer with us, but Frank's still larger than life, entertaining folks at sporting dinners with his outrageous (but very true) tales of his life in soccer. If you go to one of his do's, you can't miss him – he's the one with the Stetson, the string tie and the cowboy boots! Anyway, the following day was a golf tournament. In those days I was still able to get out and about on the course. I always liked my golf. On the Sunday a Minehead eleven took on an all-stars side which included Alan Birchenall, Geoff Merrick, Martin Buchan, Bestie, Ossie and Frank (Worthington). The following weekend Bally brought his Exeter side to play Minehead and the weekend after that, Joe brought his Oldham team down. To all intents and purposes it was going well. At one stage I was told that there was about £5,000 in the kitty. To this day, no one knows where that money went, apart from whoever took it. There were lots of fingers pointed, but nothing definite was ever made public. The trouble with something like a testimonial is that there are usually a lot of people involved and various expenses to be paid.

A few months later, despite all the setbacks and with my health not getting any better, I managed to join my old mate Ian Botham as he took part in one of his famous charity walks. I think I did over 130 miles with 'Beefy' and although I couldn't always keep up with him, I was never too far behind. It was hard – very hard – but I was determined to give it a go. During the walk we were joined by various people, including one of my old City team mates, former goalkeeper Len Bond. Alan Ball was another to link up with us and, if I remember correctly (and because of my condition, my memory is not what it was) the singer from Spandau Ballet, Martin Kemp, though I can't say I recall him singing much! As I say, it was tough going, but I wanted to prove to myself that I could do it and, at the same time, bring the plight of Parkinson sufferers into the public eye. Also, I did it for Ian. That man has got the biggest heart and what he has done to raise money for leukaemia research is brilliant. And, at a time when things were black for me, it gave me back a bit of confidence. But, as the year rolled on, life for me – and those around me – became more and more depressing. Despite the fact that money was tight, I was still gambling – safely, I thought, just a little flutter here and there – and still losing. Still taking umpteen drugs a day and trying to deal with my circumstances. Terribly depressed. I wasn't a nice person to live with. In the end I knew that things couldn't continue as they were. Trish and I were finished. It's an old cliché, but we'd grown apart, it happens to the best of marriages. It was a real body blow to reach the decision to split up, but life was hell for both of us. Twenty-five years of marriage, with good times at the start and bad times, very bad times, later. We talked it through and then broke the news to the kids. At least we'd had those good times earlier on and the best of them were our three wonderful children. Having made the decision and told the children, I decided to go. I packed a bag, just a small sports bag with a few bits and pieces and, with just £50 on me, I walked away,

Fifty pounds! Not that long ago I would have put that on a horse and not batted an eyelid. Now that was all I had in the world. But where to go? Mum's was out of the question, Dad having died not long before I finished at the Frazer Group. I wasn't going to burden her. Brother Martin had a house full in Ashton, so that was a non-starter. I found myself at Nailsea railway station and caught the train to Weston-super-Mare. I spent the night sleeping rough on the sands under the pier. I'd reached rock bottom. From staying in the best hotels and eating at expensive restaurants, I was reduced to sleeping rough. The next day, without a clue what to do next, I was walking around Weston High Street, when I bumped into John Jones, who turned out to be a real-life Good Samaritan. John had known me from my footballing days and was a Yeovil Town supporter. He could see something was badly wrong. He asked where I was sleeping, so I told him. He was shocked. 'And tonight?' 'Same place I guess,' was my answer. 'No you're not, you're coming back with me.' John lived in Yeovil and had got into the property market at the right time, buying houses, doing them up and selling them.

He put me up at one of his places, telling me I could stay as long as I wanted. In return, I helped out as a sort of builder's mate. That went on for a while and I was able to go backwards and forwards to Nailsea to see the kids.

With the divorce taking its course, I had left Trish to sort everything out. As with any marriage break-up there are dozens of things to be sorted, not least the sale of the house. Thanks to John and his kindness, I continued to stay in Yeovil for a short time, while I attempted to get my life into some sort of order. Later, when he expanded his business, I continued to help out. It was in the summer of 1990 that my luck changed very much for the better and I met Ruth. As in lots of relationships, it was a complete fluke – an act of fate if you like – that we ever met at all. I was going down to Swansea to meet up with good friend and cricket star Viv Richards and to watch the West Indies cricket team in action. I offered to take a friend called Pat to the game and she said, 'Fine, but can we pick up my best friend Ruth on the way?' And that was how I came to meet Ruth. Just for once life had dealt me a winner, my luck had changed for the better. We hit it off straight away and it was to prove to be the beginning of a fantastic relationship, which, at the time of writing, goes back eighteen years. I soon found out that Ruth knew next to nothing about cricket when we got to the game. She confused the West Indian steel band with the touring cricket team! As these things often do, we started off as friends. In fact, it was six months before I asked her out 'on a date'. I told her straight away about my illness – I could hardly keep it from her – and also about my addiction for the odd bet. She took it all in her stride. When we were first going out I would occasionally take her to the races. In fact, I even started winning a few bets. Not that that solved too many financial problems – there's no one more generous than a winning gambler. But Ruth is nobody's fool and soon realised that my gambling was a real problem.

However, there was some hope, financially, as the end of the 1993/4 season approached. I had the prospect of that testimonial with Manchester United coming up. I was hoping for a half decent crowd attendance for the game, but was gob-smacked when it turned out to be a sell out. Although Fergie couldn't be there himself, his number two, Brian Kidd, who I'd first met when I was called up for the England youth team, brought a star-studded side down that included Peter Schmeichel, Steve Bruce, Bryan Robson, Lee Sharpe, Mark Hughes and Paul Ince. Basically, it was their normal first team line up, that had just won the title. Over twenty thousand fans – a full house – packed into the ground. It was unbelievable, fantastic. The two teams lined up by the tunnel before the game to clap me onto the pitch and I came through to applaud the crowd. It was quite emotional, a memory that I will never forget. Afterwards, once the various expenses, VAT etc had been taken off, I eventually received about £81,000 from the fund-raising committee. The first thing I did was to pay off most of the mortgage on the house at Nailsea and then split the rest between Trish and the kids. But there was one sour note from the night. I'd agreed with Donnie Gillies to make a donation from the fund to the cancer unit at Bath Hospital, where Donnie's wife Ann was being treated. I knew Ann well, a lovely lady, but when I went to see her while she was in hospital, she was too poorly for visitors.

Sadly, she lost her battle. Three or four of the lads that I had played with in the City team had lost their partners in similar tragic circumstances and my heart went out to all of them. But, for some reason, Donnie was under the impression that half of the money from the game was going to the hospital, which wasn't the case. It got messy and solicitors were involved. I think Donnie was misinformed or misled. I'm no saint, but there was never any intention to split the money. And I certainly had no intention of conning Donnie. I'd always said I would give £5,000 from the game – and I did. The rest was supposed to clear debts and leave me enough to live on. I'm just so sad that it got to the stage of spoiling a good friendship.

After all the pre-and post-match publicity of the big game it was back to the day-to-day existence that I had grown used to. Parkinson's had taken over my life and it seemed to me that every time I saw the specialist I was being prescribed more and more drugs. I had all sorts of pills to take to combat the various effects of Parkinson's Disease. I had pills to help me sleep and pills to wake me up. I was on so many pills I must have rattled! It wouldn't have been so bad if I felt that they were helping me, but I was sure I was getting worse. On the plus side I had very strong support from Ruth and our friends. By this time Ruth and I were 'an item' and had set up home together in Newport. Ruth was the crutch I needed and gave me the stability and support I so desperately needed. If it wasn't for her I don't know where I'd be now. She was a real trooper, she put up with so much, even when I was asleep. Because of the Miropexin, I would have terrible nightmares, which, most nights, would end up with me thrashing about and hitting out. Ruth must have thought she was in bed with a boxing octopus! Not that Ruth is the only love of my life – I've also got Popsie and Pippie. Don't get the wrong idea. They're not a couple of ravers from the local disco, they're my two little Jack Russells. Great company and also good exercise for me when I take them out for walks.

I also got a lot of enjoyment and distraction when I decided to run a soccer skills coaching course for youngsters in Newport. That was in 1999 and we held the sessions at the Spytty Park Sports Centre. The idea was to concentrate on technique, ball control and skills. The kids loved it. I introduced them to the game of footie tennis, which is basically that – tennis, but using feet and head instead of a racket. Excellent for developing ball-control skills. I would take about a dozen youngsters at a time and, over the course of the four years I was able to run it, hundreds of kids took part. One or two promising players came through. Probably the best was a youngster called Chris Gunter. I realised straightaway he had that certain something needed to have a chance of making it in the professional game. It was no surprise when he was snapped up by Cardiff City and I used to watch him in the reserves when he first went to Ninian Park. It gave me so much satisfaction to see him playing so well. He'd grown physically and never looked out of place playing with and against older, more experienced professionals. He went on to become one of the youngest players to turn out for Cardiff City's first team and the full Welsh national team. He was very soon the attention of scouts from all the top clubs and over the Christmas period last year was sold to Tottenham for a fee of around £3million. Obviously Chris was the outstanding lad from those that came along to my sessions, but I'd like to think that I helped all the youngsters that attended and that they all learned something and enjoyed the experience. I certainly did. Psychologically it did wonders for me, but after four years I was physically unable to continue.

It was around that time that I learnt of the death of one of my old team mates at City, Chris Crowe. A very skilful footballer who'd made his name with Nottingham Forest, Wolves and England, Chris hadn't enjoyed the best of luck or health in his later years and his death, although not totally unexpected, was still a shock. I went to pay my respects at his funeral at the Bristol South Crematorium, along with a few other former City players, notably Jantzen Derrick, Mike Gibson and Gordon Parr. I think the final act of respect that you can show to someone is to attend their funeral and I found it very sad that his was not particularly well attended.

It was about a year after I had to pack in the coaching that I had a much-needed morale booster. Like all couples once they'd been together a while, I thought Ruth and I knew each other pretty well. But, in 2004, she took me by surprise. We were on a short-break holiday in a cottage in Pembrokeshire. We had just enjoyed a nice day out and were settling down for the evening with a drink when she proposed marriage. Initially I was lost for words. 'Are you sure about this?' was my response, when I finally got over the shock. Three months later we were married at The Priory Hotel in Caerleon in South Wales. We didn't want a huge wedding, just close friends and family. I knew that to invite various friends from the sports world could turn it into a bit of a sporting circus – not to mention attract the attention of the media – although I was delighted that Geoff Merrick agreed to be my best man. Ruth's son Nick was there, as well as my son Adam and daughter Jess. Unfortunately Ryan was working away and couldn't make it, but did send us a card and his love and best wishes.

Now I was a married man again it was even more important to try and do something to improve my health – not just for my quality of life, but for Ruth's as well. Believe me, terrible though it is for someone with a disease like Parkinson's, it's no fun for their partner either. But there was another more pressing problem to deal with. That was my other 'illness' – gambling. I'd always liked a flutter, but it was while I was on the dreaded Miropexin that my gambling really took over my life. That drug has had a lot of press about the terrible side effects that can occur, causing obsessive behaviour – gambling and even sex addiction. Hundreds of compensation cases have already gone through the courts. The first case in Europe was won in France recently, where 'the victim' had lost the equivalent of £90,000 gambling. As yet, nothing has happened in Great Britain, although there were three cases pending in Nottingham. Although I was now settled in Newport, I was up to my eyeballs in credit cards, milking them to the limit to feed my habit. I also had accounts with all the major bookmakers. And I also owed to money lenders, paying horrendous interest rates. My normal day revolved around betting, at any price. And not just a fiver or a tenner. I was betting silly money – £300 or £400 a day. And all the time the bills and final demands for outstanding payments would come and I would just ignore them, hide them away. I was in serious trouble. Ruth was my saviour. Her finding out just how deep I was in was what saved me. We sat down and went through everything – all the debts I had. The first thing we did was to cut up the credit cards, although Ruth went on paying my credit card bills when they came in. She did that for over a year, but it was totally unfair on her and impossible for her to continue doing it. Then we went to see our closest friends and told them the situation. I was amazed when they offered financial help – I felt so humble. To this day I would like to thank two particular friends, Viv and Steve, for repaying one of my more pressing debts, something I will never forget. Another one of our friends is a solicitor and we sought his advice. He suggested that my best course of action was to be declared bankrupt. It actually costs £400 to do that – ironic that and another bill to pass on to Ruth. So that was what I did. I went down to the insolvency courts in Newport and went through everything all over again with the local magistrate. The first thing that happens is that your bank account is frozen, closed off to you. The same with any other accounts – building society account or a credit card account and so on – that you have. Then you wait while all the details in your case are examined thoroughly and your creditors are contacted to advise them of your situation. And that's what happened to me. After a couple of weeks I had to attend an insolvency hearing at the court in Newport, where the decision was made that I was to be officially declared voluntarily bankrupt. It was probably the only decision they could have reached and was the best thing that could have happened under the circumstances.

That was about three years ago and since that time I've lived without a bank account and have as much chance of getting credit or a loan as I have of making another come-back for Bristol City! Ruth looks after all our finances – our income from her job as a manager with The Brook Street Employment Agency and my disability allowance. She makes sure the everyday bills are paid and that I've got a couple of quid (no more though) if I want to pop down the shop and buy a paper and a few odds and ends. Now that we had one of my illnesses under control, we looked at what we could do to improve things as far as the Parkinson's was concerned. We had read anything and everything that was published about the illness to see if there was light on the horizon regarding treatment. With over 120,000 people suffering from it in the UK alone there was plenty to read on the subject. But no real glimmer of hope of anything positive in terms of a cure or a major improvement in quality of life for sufferers. Then, on one of my six-monthly check-ups at Frenchay Hospital, my surgeon told me that there was a breakthrough in the treatment that could make a big difference, something called a deep brain stimulation operation.

Would I be interested?

CHAPTER NINE

UNDER THE KNIFE,
THEN BACK WITH THE LADS

A pioneering operation. A breakthrough in dramatically improving my condition, maybe even a cure. I could barely take it all in and was getting very excited. Would I be interested? Is the Pope Catholic? You bet I was interested. But I was brought down to earth with a bang. The operation was very new and certainly wasn't available on the National Health. It would cost thousands of pounds. Chris Garland, bankrupt and with no cheque book or Barclay Gold Card was hardly in a position to say; 'Fine – how would you like me to pay?' I got home and talked it through with Ruth. She suggested that the Professional Footballers Association might help. So, we got in touch with Christine Matthews, who had been secretary at Chelsea during the Seventies, to see if she could point us in the right direction. Chris was, still is, a very knowledgeable person and was always very helpful to Chelsea players, past or present, during my time with the club. Straightaway I had two determined individuals on my side, Ruth and Christine. Between them they made countless phone calls to John Barnwell, the chief executive with the Football League Managers' Association and succeeded in convincing him to support my case with the PFA for financial help to cover the cost of the operation. Thanks to him and the unstinting efforts of Ruth and Christine, the PFA agreed to fund the op and to this day, Ruth and I will always be grateful for their support.

The whole process of funding by the PFA took about four months before we were given the green light. After that I had a meeting with the surgeon, Mr Stephen Gill. He explained in detail what the operation involved. He told me that, in layman's terms, they would need to implant a stimulator, a bit like a pacemaker, approximately four inches by three, in the left-hand side of my chest. This would be connected – wired up – through the inside of the skin in my neck and connected to a large probe into my brain. There was another piece of

The 'David Soul look' at Chelsea.

A move to Leicester and a goal against Newcastle and my old team-mate keeper Jock Mahoney.

Trish, Adam and Ryan.

The new family home in Leicester.

Challenging Newcastle's Malcolm MacDonald, while Frank Worthington looks on.

Scoring at Filbert Street against Manchester City.

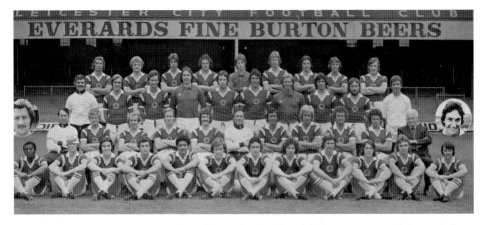

Leicester team photograph, 76/77. I'm in the third row, second from left.

In action again for Leicester. *(Leicester Mercury)*

Back at Bristol City.
(Picture Mike Jay)

Together with my hero, Mr Bristol City, John Atyeo.

A sporting dinner at The Dragonara, with Peter Osgood, George Best, Paul Cheesley, Gerry Sweeney, Geoff Merrick, Gerry Gow and Ian Hutchinson.

Off to the casino with some sporting friends. Gerry Gow, Viv Richards, Brian Rose, Ian Botham, Alan from the casino and me.

An interesting photograph this. Here I am presenting a sporting award
to young James Ryan. Nearly twenty years later, he and Mark Leesdad
helped me write this book.

What a character! Staunch City supporter
Jack Woodford at 94. He followed the
fortunes of Bristol City since he was a
youngster and would always give you
words of encouragement when you
arrived at the ground for a game.

My good friend Ian Botham signs for Yeovil, watched by manager
Gerry Gow and chairman Gerry Lock.

A toast to the ill-fated Minehead testimonial. From the left, former City
keeper John Macey, Geoff Merrick, myself and Alan Birchenall.

Celebrating my old friend Keith Goodenough's sixtieth birthday.

Together with three old City stalwarts, Brian Drysdale, Trevor Tainton and Gerry Sweeney. (Photo: Phil McCheyne Photography, Nailsea)

Back together again for the first time in twenty-five years, thanks to the
Bristol City Supporters Trust – the Ashton Gate Eight.
Back row: Peter Aitken, Julian Marshall, David Rodgers and Geoff Merrick.
Front: Gerry Sweeney, Trevor Tainton, myself and Jimmy Mann.
(Photo: Phil McCheyne Photography, Nailsea)

Still in demand for autographs, myself and David Rodgers at a
Supporters Club function.
(Photo: Phil McCheyne Photography, Nailsea)

Promoting my testimonial match with Manchester United.

Walking out on the pitch before the start of my testimonial.

Applauding the fans at Ashton Gate before my game with
Man United kicked off.

Close-up of me applauding fans at my testimonial.

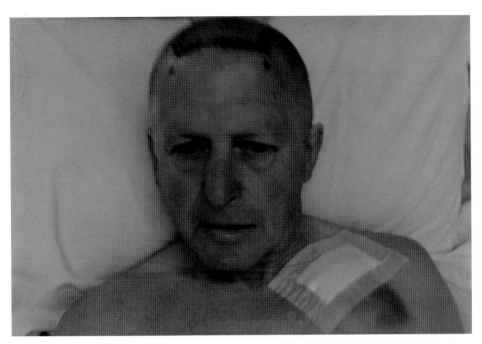

Twenty-four hours after pioneering brain surgery – not a pretty sight.

Checking out my new look, after my operation.

Daughter Jess with her brothers Adam and Ryan.

It's an early bath for grand-daughter Eva.

Meeting up with my good friend Joe Royle.

Keeping me on the straight and narrow, my wife Ruth.

(Photo: Phil McCheyne Photography, Nailsea)

equipment, a bit like a TV remote control, that I would have to place on my chest over the stimulator and, when I switched it on, it would send a charge to activate the stimulator, creating a surge through the wire to activate the brain cells needed to produce dopamine. He added that the whole operation would take six to seven hours and that I would be in hospital for about a week. If successful, Mr Gill said this could improve my quality of life by about twenty to thirty per cent, but that there were no guarantees.

Thanks to the PFA's financial support, the operation was arranged very quickly and, on 11 May 2006, Ruth drove me to Frenchay Hospital, on the outskirts of Bristol. Although I was nervous, there was never any doubt in my mind about going through with it. I would have done anything to improve my worsening health. My first day in was taken up by various pre-op checks and, understandably, it was 'nil by mouth'. It's amazing how dry your mouth gets and how thirsty you feel when you're in that situation. The nature of the operation meant I needed to have my head shaved, but I'd already turned that necessity into a virtue, by taking part in a sponsored head shave the previous Sunday, raising £170 for Mr Gill's research into Parkinson's. I also raised a further £130 for the local Parkinson's Disease Society, by going round with a collecting tin. Knowing that I'd have to have my head shaved, I felt that the charities might just as well benefit. On day two – 12 May at around mid-day – I was wheeled off to the operating theatre, son Adam and daughter Jess in close attendance. The last thing I remember as the anaesthetic took effect was seeing their faces. I didn't really know a lot about the next six or seven hours, but eventually came round feeling awful and very uncomfortable. Apart from the after-effects of the anaesthetic, I had some sort of helmet contraption screwed to my head to protect the surgeon's work. I must have looked like a cross between Herman Munster and the monster from Frankenstein. Karen O'Sullivan, the hospital's Parkinson's specialist, came to see me once the anaesthetic had worn off. She told me that the operation had gone well. I thought, well I'm still here, so it can't have been a disaster! I immediately asked if that meant I could discharge myself after forty-eight hours. Given that I had just had major brain surgery, her reply – 'I don't really think so!' – was not a total surprise. I've never liked hospitals, but I don't suppose anyone does. Over the years, I've been in a few times for treatment to football-related ailments. But I'm not the best patient in the world and

I can't wait to get out. Don't misunderstand me, I have the utmost respect for the people who work in them and the marvellous job they do – more than ever now – but I just have this thing about being in hospital. Mr Gill came to see me and was delighted with the way it was all progressing. He said that they'd found I had a 'clean brain', whatever that means. I explained it was probably down to lack of use! One of my visitors during my stay at Frenchay was former team-mate Howard Pritchard. How he managed to find me, given the fact that he could never find me with his crosses into the penalty area when we played at City, was a miracle in itself (only joking, Pritch!) By the fourth day I was feeling a lot better and was itching to get home, even with a bald head, although Ruth said that my looks had actually improved! Karen O'Sullivan was aware that I was anxious to leave – I'd got to the stage where I was thinking of forming an escape committee, as in *The Great Escape*! – and she realised she couldn't persuade me to remain in their care. As soon as (reluctantly) I was given the green light to discharge myself, I was on the phone to Ruth to ask her to pick me up.

Obviously, I was under orders to take things very easy. So it must have been fate that, when we stopped off for a newspaper, I bumped into one of my old golfing partners. He couldn't believe I was out. We were on the golf course one week after the operation, although I have to say the operation had done nothing to improve my game. I just about managed six holes before realising I couldn't complete the course. I was trying to run before I could walk – typical Chris Garland impatience. On the plus side, as the weeks went on I was feeling much better – better than I had felt for a long time. Although my walking was still inhibited, I was OK to take the dogs out and my medication was reduced from thirty to just half a dozen tablets a day.

As I continued to improve, I decided to do something positive to help the Parkinson's Research unit at Frenchay – a fund raiser in the form of a golf day. Like many footballers, I've always enjoyed a round of golf, although I'm not fanatical about it, like one or two of my old team mates, such as Sweenes (Gerry Sweeney) or Tommy Baldwin (sorry lads – I'm a fair weather golfer, give me a ring when the weather's improved!). At my best I have an official handicap of 24 – no threat to Tiger Woods, in fact, no threat to anyone. I decided to organise a big charity golfing day at Newport Golf Club at Rogerstone and invite many of my friends from the world of soccer to take part. I never realised how much is involved in organising one of these events – a hundred and one things, from booking the course to sorting out the menu. Ruth said I'd taken on too much and, as always, she was right. By the time the day came around, I was mentally knackered. Physically I was feeling the strain a bit as well so opted out of actually taking part in the game. There was a fantastic turn-out, though, and the teams teeing off read like a *Who's Who* of soccer, with Brian Clark, Gerry Sweeney, Mark Gavin, Graham Day, Geoff Twentyman, Peter Aitken, Bobby Woodruff, Gary Plumley, Martyn and Peter Rogers, Alan Dicks, Alec Briggs, Ronnie Harris and Tommy Baldwin, to name but a few. And, from the world of sporting journalism, Peter Godsiff and Roger Malone. Overall winners of the day's golfing was Alan Dicks' team of Brian Clark, Roger Malone and Peter Godsiff. I made it for the dinner, where the footballers of yesteryear swapped yarns and reminiscences. In my experience, there is no other profession in the world that has the same camaraderie as footballers. In my opinion it's unique – the jokes, the banter, the wind-ups and, when the chips are down, the genuine desire to help their mates or people worse off.

You occasionally see pictures in the paper of footballers visiting a hospital or taking part in a fund-raising game of golf or soccer, but there are hundreds of instances of players helping others that are never publicised. Still, with two 'sports hacks' in the winning team, publicity was guaranteed. Ronnie 'Chopper' Harris did the after-dinner chat and was excellent. A great bloke and a very under-rated footballer. Many people think of Ron as just one of soccer's hard men, but there was more to his game than that. (It was the same when Norman Hunter signed for Bristol City. Everyone knew how hard Norman was, his reputation preceded him, but he surprised a lot of people with his skill.) Mind you, I'm glad I never had to play against Ron during my career. I can vividly remember one needle match at Anfield – most Liverpool–Chelsea games were needle matches in those days. Ron and Liverpool's Emlyn Hughes didn't like each other very much and you knew that they would clash at some stage. About half an hour into the game there was a loose ball on the half way line. Ron came charging in and the Liverpool player ended up on the deck. Unfortunately, Ron, who is short-sighted, had got the wrong man and floored Liverpool hard man, Tommy Smith by mistake. Glancing down at the prostrate Smith, Ron, being Ron, said, 'Come on Tommy,

you're getting soft in your old age!' Tommy Smith was not amused –
steaming in fact! There weren't too many players around who could
do that to Tommy Smith and – as it were – live to tell the tale. Another
time we were playing a pre-season game in northern Spain. We had a
young full-back called Gary Locke who got badly clattered. Ron was
a great believer in the old 'eye for an eye' motto, but because of his
short-sightedness, wasn't sure who the culprit was. 'Who was that?'
he called out to Ossie. 'Number six,' was the reply. Twenty minutes
later the Spanish number six was stretchered off and justice was done.
Those are just two of the stories I could tell you about Ron and he had
plenty of similar tales to tell as the after-dinner speaker. I couldn't
help thinking that these days he'd probably be red-carded in the pre-
match warm up! Thanks to all the lads who took part – winners, losers
and story tellers – a sum of just over £1,000 was raised for the
Parkinson's charity.

   As 2006 turned into 2007, out of the blue I received a letter from
the Bristol City Supporters Trust. They were trying to organise a
special reunion dinner to commemorate the twenty-fifth anniversary
of the Ashton Gate Eight's sacrifice to save Bristol City. It was
unexpected to say the least after all that time and I was in two minds
about it. So much had happened to me since that day in February 1982
and so much had been said or written about the Ashton Gate Eight
since, that I wondered whether it should be just left in the past –
yesterday's news. If you keep looking back, you'll never look
forward. Having thought that, I decided, health permitting, that I
wanted to go. It would be good to see the lads together again.
Obviously I'd seen Geoff (Merrick) a fair bit over the previous
twenty-five years and, every now and again, 'Sweenes' (Gerry
Sweeney), Peter (Aitken), Dave (Rodgers) and, once in a while,
Trevor (Tainton). But I hadn't seen either Jimmy Mann or Julian
Marshall since we all walked away from the club. In any case, as I was
due a visit to see my mum, I could kill two birds with one stone and
pick her up on the way. I drove to the ground with Ruth, it was the
first time she'd been to Bristol City. The first person I saw as I got out
of the car was Marina Dolman, widow of the late Harry Dolman – the
best chairman Bristol City has ever had. Marina is a very genuine
person and, like Harry, Bristol City through and through. She greeted
me warmly and said that she was so pleased that I had been able to
make it. She sat with us during the evening and, knowing about my

health, was very supportive throughout the night. Another one to 'look after me' during the evening was Bristol-born champion boxer Jane Couch. 'Anyone bothers you, just let me know and I'll sort them out,' she said. Most of the other members of the eight were already there when I arrived and it was like one of those school reunions. Julian was there, a gentle giant, though I did point out that I thought he'd put on a few pounds since I'd last seen him. I heard later that he was the hardest one of the eight to track down. Jimmy Mann, who I understand was in two minds whether to come practically up until the last minute, shook hands, smiled and told me I was looking well. Mind you, a great little player, but he never was very good at lying! Jim's facial expressions always gave him away – one of the reasons why he was such a lousy card player. There was a huge turnout for the event, lots of familiar faces amongst the fans who seemed genuinely pleased that the eight were all there. One of the most nerve-racking points of the evening was doing interviews for the TV and radio people. I'd been used to doing hundreds of interviews over the years as a player, but I was concerned about how I would cope, in my present condition, with having a microphone poked in front of me and a TV camera pointed at me. I was very nervous, but I think it went OK. There was also a question-and-answer spot in the evening for each of us and, again, I was concerned how I would react. I was certainly glad when that part of the evening was over and done with. It gave us the chance, with no holds barred, to let the fans know exactly how we felt about the way we had been used and treated all those years ago, but they all knew how we must have felt long before the evening took place. The standing ovation we got when we walked into the main dining area was something I will never forget. I thought the evening was a success, even if one or two old wounds were reopened, but you can't turn the clock back and what's done is done. It was good to see all the lads again and the many supporters who attended, but I must admit, by the time we got back to Newport, I was dead on my feet.

Not long after the Ashton Gate Eight reunion, I was invited to a dinner at Chelsea. Other ex-players there on the day included Frank Blunstone, Bristolian Roy Bentley and Terry Venables. Of course 'Tel' is one of soccer's larger-than-life characters – been there, done that, got the t-shirt. A real Eastender, a great character, a very good player during his day, excellent coach and always good for a laugh.

Ruth and I went by train on one of the hottest days of the year. I must be honest, I struggled to get through it and I know I didn't cope very well – one of the reasons why I've turned down offers to go back. One of the nice things to come out of that trip was bumping into lifelong Chelsea fan and season-ticket holder Steve Faulkner. Another of life's genuine characters, he was aware of my problems and, at the end of the get-together, treated me and Ruth to a weekend away in Dorset. A really nice gesture.

As a lifelong Bristol City supporter, as well as a former player who made something like 250 senior appearances in my three spells at the club, one thought did strike me after the Ashton Gate Eight reunion. If I could put a City 'dream team' together, from all the players that had been at Ashton Gate during my playing days, what would be the line up? Eventually, I came up with this squad: Mike Gibson, Tony Ford, Brian Drysdale, Jack Connor, Norman Hunter, Geoff Merrick, Gary Collier, Gerry Gow, Jantzen Derrick, Gerry Sweeney, Johnny Quigley, Trevor Tainton, Tom Ritchie, Jimmy Mann, John Atyeo, Paul Cheesley, Brian Clark, John Galley and Clive Whitehead. I have cheated a little bit by including 'Big John' Atyeo in my team, as one of my biggest regrets in soccer is that I never got to play alongside him in the first team. But I was on the books as a youngster when John was in his prime, so I think he qualifies – especially as John's name would be the first on my team sheet, no matter which era we were looking at. For my final eleven see the end of this chapter and see if you agree with my choice. I have also had plenty of time to look back at the various managers I've played for and have come up with my personal thoughts on each of them:

Fred Ford – my first manager and the most honest and straight man I've met in football. Not a man prone to haggling. 'Fifteen pounds a week, take it or leave,' he said, when I went in to 'negotiate' my first professional contract. I took it.

Les Bardsley – the City's long-serving physio who always stepped into the breach when the club was between managers. Very much a gentleman, I was indebted to Les for giving me my first start of the season, following Fred Ford's sacking.

Alan Dicks – although I didn't always see eye to eye with Alan, I have the utmost respect for what he achieved at the club.

Ron Suart and Wilf McGuinness – in charge of the English Football Association side that toured Australia, Ron was very much 'old school' management. Wilf, on the other hand, was very hyper, a great character and a real joker – one of the lads. He told us on one occasion that there was a midnight curfew, so anyone coming back from a night out after then should use the back door!

Dave Sexton – a fantastic coach, who improved my game one hundred per cent. Not so sure that he was cut out for managing players.

Eddie McCreadie – had the thankless task of stepping up from being one of the lads to becoming manager. Mad as a hatter, but a nice bloke. Tried to persuade me not to move from Chelsea.

Jimmy Bloomfield – a very religious man, Jimmy was a very good coach. Suspect eyesight though – said he never saw what happened when I clobbered teammate Jeff Blockley, even though he was stood just a few feet away!

Alan Dicks (second time around) – having got Bristol City into the top flight, he kept them there for four years, even if he didn't keep all his promises.

Bob Houghton – all done by the book: The Bob Houghton Coaching and Management Manual. Not on my Christmas card list.

Roy Hodgson – see Bob Houghton.

Terry Cooper – always treated me well and I was so pleased he did so well for Bristol City.

I also gave some thought about the toughest defenders I've come up against in my career – and, believe me, there were some hard 'so-and-sos' about. And you must remember, these were the days long before you got red-carded just for looking as though you were thinking about committing a foul! I've narrowed my choice down to three:

Charlie Hurley – centre-half with Sunderland and Bolton. Came up against him as a young professional and he soon let young Garland know he was there.

George Curtis – centre-half with Coventry and Villa. The 'Iron Man.' Let you know 'early doors' that he was around. I'm sure he could snap a man in two without breaking sweat.

Dave Mackay – barrel-chested defender who played for Spurs and Derby. The hardest tackler I ever came across.

My 'supporter of the team' award would go to Jack 'Shaker' Woodford, who started supporting the side as a young schoolboy and was still cheering the lads on when he was well into his nineties. A former newspaper seller, Jack would always come over with a few words of encouragement when you arrived at the ground, often followed by the request; 'Don't suppose you've got a spare ticket for the game?'

Now, that all-time City line up. I didn't even consider having two goalkeepers in my squad, 'Gibbo' was by far the best I've known at City, though Tony Cook and Jan Moller were pretty good. At the back I'd have 'Sweenes', Jack Connor, Norman Hunter and 'Speedy' Drysdale. In the middle of the park I'd pick 'Gowie', Jimmy Mann, Johnny Quigley and Jantzen (Derrick). And the partner up front for 'Big John'? I finally went with 'Clarkie' (Brian Clark). And the chances are, I will probably change my mind a dozen times before this book is published, so I'm going to move on to my final chapter, before I do.

CHAPTER TEN

REFLECTIONS

As I look back now on my life, putting it all down in black and white by way of this book, I realise that today – 17 July – is our anniversary. Eighteen years ago exactly, I first met Ruth. A chance encounter, I suppose just as many relationships start off. If the West Indies hadn't been playing in Swansea… if I hadn't fancied going to the game…if Pat hadn't asked if we could pick up her best friend in Newport…if – one of the smallest words in the English dictionary and one of the biggest words in life. A hell of a lot of water has run under the bridge since that day. If fate hadn't brought us together, I'd hate to think where I'd be today, or what I'd be doing. Or even if I'd still be alive. I owe so much to so many people, and I'm not talking about money, though God knows I owed a lot of that. But, of all the people that have been there for me and helped me, I owe the most to Ruth. She has stood by me, helped me through my darkest days and given me a reason for living. Ruth, like her mother, has a very positive outlook on life and some of that has rubbed off on me. I can't wait for the day she retires in eighteen months' time, when we can spend more time together. One area that I won't be much help with, though, is the garden. Thanks to Ruth we have a lovely garden, but I'm not at all green-fingered and can just about cut the grass! Some would say that's perfectly natural, as a lot of my goals were 'daisy cutters'!

These days I get so much pleasure from the simple things in life. For example, we – Ruth, her sister Kay and I – take a trip every second Sunday to visit Ruth's mum Edna and her partner Wally in Pontypool, just half an hour's drive away, for a family Sunday lunch. What a cook! Edna produces the most marvellous traditional Sunday lunch. (Fortunately, being a good cook is just one of the many attributes Ruth has inherited from her mum.) Fit as a fiddle and a very determined lady, Edna looks after three horses – point-to-pointers – even though she is in her late eighties. Occasionally, we will also meet up with Ruth's son Nick. He lives in Oxford with wife Erica and runs a recruitment business.

On the Garland side of the family, Mum still lives in the flats overlooking the City ground, although the view's not what it was before the Dolman Stand was built and both Del Boy and Chris Garland have long since vacated Nelson Mandela House! On the other hand, with concerts now being staged at the ground, she has a perfect location to listen to the music – lovely jubbly. She enjoyed Neil Diamond, but wasn't quite so keen on The Who! My eldest son Adam lives in Thornbury, near Bristol, with his girlfriend Ann. Ironically, given my problems, he had been working as a manager at one of the country's leading bookmakers until recently, but has since returned to work in the sports industry with a major golf accessory company.

My youngest son, Ryan, presented me with a granddaughter (Eva) last April, my first grandchild. A manager for a recruitment agency in the building trade, he met his wife Kerry while on a working holiday in New Zealand. Ryan from Bristol and Kerry from Forfar in Scotland and they met in New Zealand – tell me there's no such thing as fate.

Sometimes, despite having Parkinson's, you do see the funny side of things – which is just as well. When we flew up to Scotland last year for their wedding, I made a point of seeking out one of the officials at Bristol Airport to let them know about my implant. I was concerned that it might set the alarm off when we went through security and I had this vision of armed police rushing over, thinking they had a major security alert on their hands!

Daughter Jess lives just outside Bristol in Portishead, when she's home that is. As the co-assistant coach for the England Under-21 netball team, Jess has travelled extensively. She has previously represented her country at all levels and, when she's not away on international duty, coaches netball at the University of Bath.

Brother Martin lives in Ashton with his wife Barbara. An expert carpenter – unlike his brother – Martin has never been out of work in his life – again, unlike his brother, although that will all change soon, as he's due to retire. I suspect though that he'll be kept busy giving family and friends the benefit of his skills long after he's officially hung up his carpenter's apron. Sadly, his mother-in-law Eileen, who lives in London, is also a Parkinson's sufferer.

I was looking back through some of my old football programmes the other day and it struck me how many of the players I admired or played with, or, in many cases, ate, drank and gambled with, are no longer around. Characters at Chelsea like ' Ossie' and Ian Hutchinson. Without a doubt, Peter was the best centre-forward I ever played with. He had everything a centre-forward should have and very few centre-halves liked playing against him. He was always good to me and we became very good friends. Peter would often pick me up in his Jag to go training. Chelsea through and through, I know how saddened he was at being transferred to Southampton, even though he enjoyed success there and helped them to win the FA Cup. After his retirement he went on the after-dinner circuit telling outrageous football stories – and all of them true! His sudden death at a family funeral two years ago came as a great shock.

Ian 'Hutch' Hutchinson was another lovely fella. I joined Chelsea as he was fighting to recover from the same type of knee injury that finished Paul Cheesley's career and, like Paul, his footballing days were ended prematurely.

Another old Chelsea team-mate whose life was tragically cut short is Peter Houseman. A very unassuming, modest man, 'Nobby,' as he was known at the club, had come up through the youth ranks at Chelsea, making around 300 appearances for the club, before finishing his playing days with Oxford United. He was terribly under-rated and the best crosser of a ball I have played with. Sadly, he was killed in a car crash, along with wife Sally and two friends, leaving their three young children orphaned. Such a waste.

Of course, you can't talk about top-flight football without reference to one of the very best – George Best. A great player and a good friend, what can I say about 'Bestie' that hasn't already been said? For me, still the best British player of all time and easily in the top six best in the world (Pele would be my number one – cue pub debate!).

At Leicester, one of the most skilful players during my time there was Keith Weller. Like Ossie, Keith was devastated when he left Chelsea, but soon became a star performer for Leicester. A great person on and off the pitch, he was also my golfing partner during my time with 'The Foxes'. Keith finished his playing days in the United States but, after a number of operations, lost his battle with cancer in 2004.

Of course, there were some great characters, sadly no longer with us, at Bristol City. People like 'Cookie' (Tony Cook), Bobby Etheridge, Jimmy Rogers and Mike Thresher – what an apt surname for Mike's style of play at full-back. Do you know, he once marked the great Stanley Matthews out of a game at Ashton Gate and then popped in the away dressing room to get Stan to sign his programme. During my first-team days at City there was Johnny Quigley. A lovely bloke and an excellent team captain, John always looked out for the younger players, including me. An excellent trainer and a good pro, John loved the West Country and was upset when his time in Bristol came to an end and he was transferred to Mansfield. After finishing his playing career there, he had spells coaching in England and the Middle East. News of his death in 2004 came as a big shock.

And the greatest of them all at Ashton Gate – John Atyeo. That man was my inspiration to become a footballer and was the best player ever to pull on a Bristol City shirt. From getting his autograph as a young boy, to cleaning his boots as an apprentice and, ultimately, to putting on the same number 8 shirt for Bristol City. Although I regret not playing in the first team alongside the great man, I got to see him many times after his retirement from football. I attended his funeral when he so sadly died at the age of sixty-one in 1993. The church in his home town of Warminster – the same church where he had been married all those years before – was packed to the ceiling – with so many of his old team mates, including Jack Boxley, who had been his best man all those years before, coming to pay their last respects. There weren't many dry eyes that day, especially when they played Bristol City's signature tune 'When the Red Red Robin Comes Bob Bob Bobbin' Along' at the end of the service. John, if you're looking down on me, I'd like to say that you set your standards too high for me. I was only 261 goals behind you, but more than a few bookings and sendings off ahead of you! (For those of you who didn't know, John Atyeo was never booked or sent off in his career.)

Looking through those old programmes also got me thinking about all the grounds that I played on – I must have appeared at all the original Football League grounds at some stage or another. Like all footballers, I had my favourite grounds and my least favourite. Among the ones I enjoyed most is White Hart Lane, partly because I scored there to help Chelsea reach the final of the League Cup. Old Trafford is another that gets my vote, one of the best grounds in the country and a fantastic atmosphere. Villa Park also gets the 'Chris Garland Seal of Approval', if just for their fantastic dressing-rooms that always had plenty of fancy soaps and shampoos – essential for putting the Garland barnet back into shape after a game! And finally, Fratton Park, home of Portsmouth. Probably the best playing surface in the League in my day. It was such a good pitch that it often worked against the home side, as visiting teams looked forward to playing on it.

And the worst grounds! Well, there was Derby's old home, The Baseball Ground. I swear they used to water that pitch every home match, no matter what time of year it was. A real mud heap. The Old Den was a very intimidating place to play, you needed waterproofs to protect you from the fans spitting, while St Andrews, home of Birmingham City, was another ground I didn't like, mainly because I don't recall ever having a good game there. And finally, Darlington's old home turf – Feethams. OK, I did score my last-ever League goal there, but the place really was from a bygone era and falling to bits. Someone joked that even squatters wouldn't stay there! I'm pleased for their fans that they've since moved on to a modern, purpose-built stadium.

On the subject of locations, it also struck me that I've been fortunate to have travelled all over the globe, thanks to life as a professional footballer. In fact, I must have been round the world twice. Holland and Sweden were both nice places, clean and friendly. I didn't really get to see a lot of Germany. It was a case of airport-hotel-ground-hotel-airport. Spain I found to be hot, dry and sweaty, Norway was very nice, but I did regret flying through the mountains in a small aircraft while there – I might have been good in the air, but I'm not so good that high up with mountains either side of me! Barbados was beautiful, while Magaluf was a bit like Blackpool, but with sun! Hong Kong is like the rush-hour here, but twenty-four hours a day, while you can't help but have a nice day in the United States. Canada was fabulous, absolutely breath-taking. And probably my favourite of them all, Australia. Golden beaches, blue seas, clean – a really beautiful country.

So what of Chris Garland now? Well, as I've said, I'm looking forward to spending more time with Ruth. As far as my illness is concerned, I have to have regular assessments to monitor the Parkinson's and, in about three years time, I will need to have a replacement stimulator, at a cost of around £5,000, though by that time, with the way inflation's going, it could well be a lot more. Hopefully, with the PFA having put up the outlay for the original implant and so on, I'll be able to get that on the National Health. Of course, there's always the hope that one day they'll find a cure for this horrible illness and my surgeon, Mr Gill, was optimistic that a cure would be found – something that I and every other sufferer prays for.

I spent the first half of my life achieving my boyhood dreams. If someone had told me when I was a lad that I would play for the team that I supported; clean my hero's boots; go on to earn big-money transfers to Chelsea and Leicester; wear the Three Lions shirt; score regularly against the best teams in the country – the Arsenals, the Leeds, the Man Uniteds – and come home to play for City again in the top division, I would never have believed it could possibly happen. By the same token, if someone had predicted when I was at the peak of my career that the club that I love would ask me to tear up my contract in order for it to survive; that I would consider suicide; sleep rough; become bankrupt, be addicted to gambling; be made redundant and become a victim to a horrible disease such as Parkinson's, I couldn't possibly have believed that any one of those things, never mind all of them, could possibly happen to me. Can you imagine a fortune teller coming up with those sort of predictions the day after I'd played at Stamford Bridge or Wembley, or had just rubbed shoulders with the rich and the famous at some posh restaurant in the King's Road – it was unthinkable.

Despite everything that has happened to me in the last twenty-five years, I consider myself to have been very lucky. It's practically every schoolboy's dream to make it as a professional footballer and enjoy all the benefits and experiences that go with that. I suppose the only part of my footballing days that I do regret was my naivety when it came to contract negotiations. For example, signing a blank contract at Chelsea. And, even with the pay rise that went with the move, it never struck me that the cost of living in London, particularly the mortgage, would more than wipe out the increase in wages. When I moved on to Leicester, I should have talked to Everton, who came in with a late bid to sign me. And, when I returned home to Bristol City, I signed for the same money that I was on at Leicester and even paid my own removal fees. Now I'm not a big fan of agents, but I'm sure that if I'd had one in those days, I would certainly have done better financially. But, on the other hand, I loved practically every minute of being a professional footballer (obviously excluding the crash of '82). Thanks to football, I've met some fantastic people, on and off the pitch, forged some real friendships that will last a lifetime and travelled the world. Yes, I consider myself to have been lucky.

Ruth said the other day that it's better to be born lucky than born rich and she's right. In many respects I have been luckier than lots of people in this world. As I said earlier, she's a very positive woman – her glass is always half full, not half empty. I have enjoyed all the good times and I've come through the bad times that came my way. Basically, it's been a life of two halves – and it's not over yet.

INDEX

ALSO BY REDCLIFFE PRESS

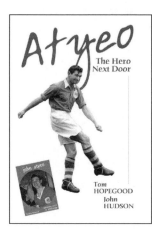

ATYEO: THE HERO NEXT DOOR
Tom Hopegood and John Hudson

When John Atyeo died in 1993, his former team-mate Jimmy Rogers said: 'They broke the mould after they made him.' It is the kind of tribute paid to the recently deceased often enough, but rarely has it rung more true than in the case of Big John, whose 350 Football League and Cup goals and 597 League appearances for Bristol City will almost certainly never be surpassed.

In his playing days, John Atyeo was a by-word for one-club loyalty and for fair play, but as Tom Hopegood and John Hudson have discovered through intensive research and interviews with family, friends and colleagues, he was much more complex than that. Readers will put this book down feeling they know the man much better than they would ever have dreamed possible.

272 pages (inc. 32pp plate section)   hardback   £17.50

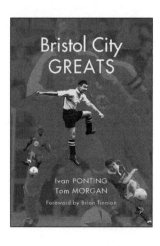

BRISTOL CITY GREATS
Ivan Ponting and Tom Morgan

Since the war, the Robins have experienced highs and lows in all four divisions of the Football League, including a heady four-year sojourn among the elite under Alan Dicks in the late 1970s.

Through it all, scores of exciting footballers have treated the Ashton Gate faithful to some fabulous entertainment. In this book – a complete update of a bestseller from 1990 – Ivan Ponting and Tom Morgan, who have both monitored Bristol soccer since their childhoods, profile City's most illustrious post-war heroes.

They are all here, from the 1940s favourites to the leading lights of recent seasons – from Roberts and Atyeo to Galley and Garland, Ritchie and Gow, Murray and Lita.

Bristol City Greats is a warm and fascinating tribute to outstanding games and much-loved personalities.

160 pages   softback   £9.99

LIFE AFTER BRISTOL CITY
Mark Leesdad
In addition to helping Chris Garland with his story, Mark Leesdad has been busy compiling *Life After Bristol City: Volume 2*.

He has personally interviewed all the former Robins in the book, discussing with them their personal experiences and stories from their footballing careers and what life had in store for them after professional soccer. In addition to such Ashton Gate favourites as Joe Royle, Jack Connor and Gerry Gow, the book will include a number of ex-City stars such as Steve Stacey, Trevor Morgan, Ken Wimshurst and Steve Neville, who now live overseas.

The new book, which will have 'then and now' photographs of all the former players, is based on his popular 'Memory Lane' series (featured each week in the *Sunday Independent*) and will be published by Redcliffe Press in 2009.

For further information, or to place an order, please contact Redcliffe Press:
T: 0117 9737207 or visit our website www.redcliffepress.co.uk